D1687338

SÜMELA
MONASTERY

by
Hasan Aydın

REPUBLIC OF TURKEY
MINISTRY OF CULTURE AND TOURISM PUBLICATIONS

© **Republic of Turkey Ministry of Culture and Tourism**
Directorate General of Libraries and Publications
3462

Handbook Series
42

ISBN: 978-975-17-3797-7

www.kulturturizm.gov.tr
e-mail: yayimlar@kulturturizm.gov.tr

Translated by
Alev Kerimoğlu Bulut

Redacted by
Okan Arslan

Photographs
Hasan Aydın

Production
MRK
Address: Batı Sitesi Mah. Gersan Sanayi Sitesi 2310 Sok. No:15
Batıkent/Yenimahalle/Ankara
Phone: 0 312 354 54 57
Web: www.mrkbaski.com
E-mail: info@mrkbaski.com
Pre-Printing: Orient Publishing (Ezgi Zorlu)

First Edition
Print Run: 5,000
Printed in Ankara in 2015.

Aydın, Hasan
Sümela Monastery / Hasan Aydın; Trans. Alev Kerimoğlu Bulut; Photos. Hasan Aydın.- Ankara: Ministry of Culture and Tourism, 2015.
144 p.: col. ill.; 19 cm.- (Ministry of Culture and Tourism Publications; 3462, Handbook Series of Directorate General of Libraries and Publications; 42)
ISBN: 978-975-17-3797-7
I. title. II. Kerimoğlu Bulut, Alev. III. series.
726.5095632515

Contents

Note on Usage

Modern Turkish uses the Latin alphabet, modified to ensure that there is a separate letter for each main sound. The spelling thus aims at ensuring phonetic consistency. For Turkish artists, names of locations, publications and special terms, this book employs modern Turkish spelling. Proper names have been kept in modern Turkish with one exception - Istanbul has been rendered with normal English spelling using I rather than İ unless it is part of a title. Consonants have more or less the same sound as in English, except for:

c like **j** in English.

ç like **ch** in English.

ğ the "soft g". Depending on the adjoining letters, this is dropped, pronounced like **y** in English, or treated a lengthening of the preceding vowel.

ı is a back, close, unrounded vowel which does not exist in English, the nearest equivalent being the phantom vowel in the second syllable of rhythm.

ö like **ö** in German or **eu** in French peur.

ş like **sh** in English.

ü like **ü** in German or u in French.

Introduction

Some places are special. Even a picture or an account of a certain place by someone who has been there, makes it occupy a special place in peoples' minds. Sumela is one of those special places. Sumela is a venue where the Orthodox believers from Anatolia, Caucasus, Russia and Greece make plans of participating in the special Sumela Service at least once in their life time. What makes this place, where Jesus Christ (AS) and Virgin Mary never sat foot, important for the believers? There are several churches in Anatolia similar to Sumela.[1] What differentiates Sumela from the others? Is it the Icon of Virgin Mary made by Saint Lucas, that is esteemed as sacred by the Orthodox believers or the Stavrotek or Ayazma symbolizing the Holy Trinity of Christianity with its triple drops? The answer for this may also be found in the location of Sumela. Resembling a gigantic black lump of a rock settled on green mountains with the look of a light coloured mark on its eastern wall, Sumela has a transcendent and innocent appearance from aside as fresh as a young bride. It is not easy at all to get closer. One has to pass beyond the steep cliff where the monastery is seen with all its grandeur as if representing the unsurpassable supremacy of the Holy Virgin.

Both the story of the founding of the monastery and the information about the early settlers and the period of settlement are not exactly known. Sumela is believed to have landed on the walls of Karadağ like a flying painting. It is a divine gift from God to mankind in respect of its location, view and water. Sumela ceased to serve in 1923 at the end of a process that lasted for centuries. Years later, in 1962, it was officially reopened to visitors and came back to life. The number of visitors increases year by year.

It is almost impossible to find a source written on Sumela that can go beyond the level of making observational views. The studies by Prof. Semavi Eyice and Dr. Hamiyet Özen have an academic value. Since Prof. Eyice's study on Sumela Monastery is the first and most comprehensive research conducted to date, it has been cited and quoted in all the studies carried out regarding the Monastery. Therefore, we decided to set out on the basis of the study by the esteemed professor and came up with the text that you will read below.

LOCATION

Sumela Monastery is located in the Maçka District of Trabzon. It is located inside Altındere Valley National Park which received an official national park status in 1987. The monastery is located within the borders of Altındere Village and is situated at a

Figure 1- Sumela from the South

distance of 17 km. to Maçka and 47 km. to Trabzon. The group of the buildings within the monastery structure was founded on a hollow on the eastern wall of Karadağ, 300 m. high from the ground and overlooking the Altındere valley. It was also publicly called the Monastery of Meryemana (Mother Mary). The territory of the premises is the property of the Ministry of Culture and Tourism (fig.1).

Figure 2- Road to Sumela and Altındere Valley

Figure 3- Walking path

The National park, i.e. the monastery, can be accessed via the Trabzon-Erzurum State Highway (E-97) by taking a turn through the exit of the center of the District of Maçka. The road leads to Altındere Valley passing through Altındere Village first and then reaches the premises of the national park. It takes rather a short duration of 40 minutes from Trabzon to the national park area. Mass transportation vehicles are available from Trabzon to Sumela Monastery bringing the visitors to the area where the Sumela Social Center is located. The visitors are picked up by the vehicles and transported to the area where the Social Center is located. Beyond that point, the road is too narrow for the passage of the large vehicles. That is why it takes another 5 km. for the mini buses inside the National Park area, which is 250-300 m. close to the Monastery (fig.2).

There is a walkway of 1.170 m. from the Social Center to the Monastery. The road is inclined and quite steep. On the all green walking path prepared for the visitors among the high trees, 900 guardrails were placed on both sides considering the safety of the walkers (fig.3).

ORIGINS OF SUMELA'S NAME

Many sources tell that the name Sumela was derived from the word "black". These sources mention the coined word "Sumela" which bears the meaning of the Greek Mela/ Melas. The difference here is related with what the adjective black qualifies. Some sources tell us that the word "black" referred to the colour of the mountain where the monastery was settled.The name of the rocky lumpy mountain on the Kalkanlı Mountains (formerly called the Zigana), where the monastery was founded, is Karadağ. In Modern Greek, Karadağ is used as "Stoumela" and in the Greek dialect spoken in the region, the name is used as "Sou-mela". On the other hand, in other sources, the theory on the origin of the name was based on the depiction of Mary in the icon of the monastery which was said to have been made by Saint Luke. It was stated that the name Sumela was given to the Monastery due to the dark colour of the icon, even black or blackened in a way making it unrecognizable. The icon was considered the most sacred piece in the monastery (fig.4).

The most interesting suggestion for the name of Sumela was put forth by Bilge Umar:

> *"Sumela (Soumela in Hellenistic form) does not have any meaning in the Hellenic language. This name, I believe, definitely comes from the language of Cappadoccia and Su(wa)-M(a)-Ela was derived from the elements "Holy-Mother-Passage". The name of Meles Stream in Izmir which provides the passage to Halkapınar Lake -the sacred worshipping area of the Mother Goddess-, from the sea (inner corner of Izmir Gulf) by boats, and reaches out to the sea passing from the lake, is in*

Figure 4- Sumela from the North

fact derived from Mela…The passage that the name Sumela, "Holy Mother's Passage", refers to is, of course, the Valley of Meryemana (Mother Mary) Stream that serves as a natural passage above the cliff where Sumela Monastery is located. Since Mela/Melas means "dark cloured, brunette, black" in Greek, the Greeks believed that the name Sumela derived from that word; Ömer Şen (Sumela, Trabzon 1998, p.7) refers to that argument accepting it as if it reflects the reality. Yet, Sumela, as a whole, (Soumela in Hellenistic scripts)does not have any meaning in neither old nor new Hellenic language." (Bilge Umar,Karadeniz Kappadokia'sı(Pontus),Inkılap Pub.p.130)

GEOGRAPHICAL CHARACTERISTICS OF THE REGION

Sumela Monastery is the main landmark of Altındere Valley National Park which is located in the Maçka District of Trabzon, followed by the flora, fauna, geomorphological features, natural beauties and the recreational facilities of the area (fig.5).

The altitude of the National Park from the sea level ranges from 1050 m. (in the basin of Altındere Valley) to 2820 m. (at Taşkesen Hill on the southwest). Altındere forms up a deep cleave in the middle of the National Park preparing a basin with a relative altitude of around 1800 m. The co-existence of the high mountainous areas and the deep valleys is among the most unique (geomorphological) aspects of the National Park. The park area becomes higher towards the South, displaying the feature of a plateau with less inclines. Actually, the altitude of the Monastery reaches 1200 m., while the District of Maçka situated at a distance of 17 km. to the north of the Monastery, that is reached through the stateway from Trabzon, has an altitude of 17 km. This fact clearly shows how inclined the topographic structure of the site is.

The site in which Sumela Monastery is located has a rich formation of forests due to the rain and climatic conditions as it is observed in the general outlook of the rest of the Eastern Black Sea region where the National Park is found. Around 901 acres of the park area, the total of which is 4800 acres, is made of forests. These

Figure 5- Looking from bottom of slope

woods are constituted by various zones of large leaved and pine leaved trees.

Thc interesting and unsurpassably beautiful flora of Altındere Valley National Park displays a breathtaking view. Moreover, the tags with the Latin and Turkish names on the trees along the path that reaches Sumela Monastery is a positive aspect in terms of informing the visitors about the nature.

REASONS OF FOUNDING AND THE IMPORTANCE OF THE MONASTERY

There is no definite story that the historians can tell us about the founding of the Monastery. Nevertheless, what A. Mican Zehiroğlu wrote in his article entitled "Prokopius' Travel to Trabzon" needs to be considered as a text produced in accordance with the historical account. The article refers to a community called the "Tsani" who lived in the area and were described in Prokopius' words as Barbarians who lived in an isolated manner among themselves like wild animals without the possibility of being in good terms with their neighbours. The Tsani area (today's Trabzon and environs), was important. Because of that, during the conflict between Byzantine Emperor Justinanus and the Persians (527 AD), an effort was exerted to assimilate the local people and convert them into Christianity as well as rendering the widespread use of Greek (the official language of the church). They opened roads in the mountains for this purpose and rolled the inclines to make the paths stabilized enough for the passage of the horses. Thus, the Tsani people found the opportunity of establishing good relations with their neighbours and other (normal) people around. In accordance with the strategy behind the efforts for civilizing the community, "Skhamalinihi church which was stated to be constructed in Tsani land, may be the origin of today's Sumela Monastery"[2]. This seems to be the only tangible record as regards the foundation of the church and the monastery beyond the legends (fig.6).

Figure 6- Main Church is the center of complex

Another story of founding is a rumour which is used as a reference very frequently and thus needs to be told here although it is not valued highly by the historians. The information coming from the community of the monastery dates to the founding of Sumela back to very early times. Some of the Western writers who visited Sumela and its community refer to the setting of the first seeds of foundation in the 4th century. Konstantinos Fotiadis[3] tells that Sumela was founded in 386. The writer makes reference to the legend of founding that was widespread among the Christian community who lived in the area in history which was also an issue repeated in the Greek sources written regarding the monastery. According to that story, the foundations of the Monastery were laid at the time of Theodosius (January 11, 347- January 17,395) and the Monastery was restructured in the 6th century by Commander Belisarius during the time of the Emperor Justinianus. During the time of the Byzantine Emperor Justinianus (527-565) the Monastery was attached great importance. Its development started during the time of that Emperor. Justinianus gave the gift of a silver chest to the monastery as well as the manuscripts of books. It is interesting to note that this event coincided with Zehiroğlu's account of the foundation story cited in the studies of Prokopius.In 640, the rubbers plundered the valuable things in the monastery and the rest were burnt in the fire. In 644, the monks of the monastery had the place restored and transformed it back into its earlier form with the support of the surrounding regions.

The following legend may be helpful to explain how the monastery became a center of faith. According to the sacred belief of the Eastern Church, out of sixty portraits of the holy virgin made by Saint Luke, only the three originals have survived our day and have naturally been preserved in the Greek Orthodox region. The first one of these is exhibited in the big cave monastery in Mora. The second one is the property of Kikkos Monastery in Cyprus. The third one (the one that the artist loved the most and carried with him all around the world during his travels) is 'Çekirge Meryem' found here in Sumela with the unsurpassable beauty of the air and tranquility of the forests of the Black Sea (fig.7).

Figure 7- Çekirge Meryem

The legend recorded how the piece that came from the first eras of Christianity was saved from all the accidents that it went through as a mercy of God as well as its being brought to Boeotia and Athens by an heir of Saint Luke after his death. And again the legend tells in detail, how it stayed in a special house of God with the help of miracles and was esteemed and appreaciated by the community of the city of Tesau as the most powerful amulet. Yet, the portrait was transported from the temple in Acropolis where it was kept without any human help and effort, and brought to the uninhabited forests on the southeast of Trabzon. Before setting out, Mary invited two young believers, Sofronius and Barnabas to the journey from Athens to the Black Sea. These two Athenians were enchanted by the mystical beauty, and according to the sources of Piksites a high cave in a rock and the missing portrait among the green forests and the waterfalls were found to be far from all the human settlements. The cave became wider and a chapel and cottages for the two Athenian hermits were built in it. According to this legend, this endevour is the starting point of the Virgin Mary Monastery in Sumela which flourished in a little while with its size, riches and miracles. Nowhere in the world is a better match for a place of pilgrimage with such mood of faith and piousness than the evergreen and enchanting landscape of the Melas Mountain in the Black Sea.

If we leave its legends aside, the Monastery was among the earliest churches and monasteries in the world established by the Orthodox community for the purpose of disseminating Christianity in the region and recruiting the people of the region both for military and religious services.Given its trait as the oldest of its kind, the presence of the Sacred Icon by Saint Luke and the sacred bath (ayazma) gave it a reputation as a place of pilgrimage.

Virgin Mary Monastery built inside a cave in a steep cliff is a real wonder of the world with its altitude of 300 m. high above a valley the skirts of which are covered with forests. Its common name is Sumela Monastery. Its original name is "Panaghia tou Melas" which means "Virgin of Karadağ". It is also called "the Monastery inside the clouds". Mina Urgan acts as the spokesperson of the visitors in her following remarks:

> *"I also fell in love with Sumela Monastery close to Trabzon where the beauty of the nature was amazingly combined with the power of imagination of the mankind. My professor Sabahattin Eyüboğlu who was from Trabzon told about this unbelievable monastery which was carved on a mountain slope many times. He was not exaggerating anything about it at all. One could not believe his eyes upon seeing it for real."*

Visiting certain places, feeling that atmosphere gives you an ecstatic mood, an emotional uplifting. This is like the feeling of surrender as in Mecca and Jerusalem. At first sight Sumela creates the same impression on the people. There would be no Sumela without that black mountain behind it but those who look at Sumela do not see the mountain at all. All is perceived as Sumela and the precipice below. And it is always the same question asked: 'How on earth could they build this structure here?'(fig.8)

Sumela was visited by Christians and Muslims as a safe haven against the disasters just is the case in other churches and monasteries elsewhere. The icon in it was the main reason why the monastery was visited by Christians and Muslims.The rumours and legends that were summarized above were created as a result of the mission of Christianity and were imposed on the

Figure 8- Rocks where the Monastery was built on

people as they were repeated all the time. The legends help to date the history of such places much earlier in the history. And this process of creating legends is not unique to Sumela; therefore it is only one of the many similar examples. Even the Western scientists who are close at heart to Christian and Greek cultures seem to refuse these legends. We need to talk about, at this point, the "sacred" icon that is esteemed highly as mentioned above.

IMPORTANCE OF THE MONASTERY FOR BELIEVERS AND INHABITANTS OF THE REGION

The importance of the monastery can be told in two respects as for its community and for the inhabitants of the region: The perception of the Monastery by the believers is important both religiously and as a source of healing. What we meant above by the inhabitants of the region was the perception of the monastery by the Muslims which again emanates from the perception of the Monastery both in religious aspects and as a source of healing. The value attached to it is not disclaimed due to the presence of Virgin Mary in the holy book of Koran. This is because, Christianity is considered a religion with a holy book and order is given to Muslims in Koran: *"O, You who believe! Believe in Allah and His Messenger and the Book which He sent down to His Messenger and the Book which He sent down before"*. In this respect, the two quotations below will further reinforce the above-mentioned view by shedding light to the importance and traditional value of the monastery both in the lives of the Sumela community before 1923 and in the lives of the local people after the fire in 1929.

In his book entitled *the History of Trabzon (Trabzon Tarihi)* Ömer Şenin tells about the feast in 1913 as follows:

> *""Holy Virgin Feast" (Kutsal Bakire Yortusu) was held in Sumela Monastery on the 15th of August each year. All Christians in the Black Sea region wished to visit this Monastery which is one of the oldest monuments of the Christian world, to fulfill their pilgrimage service at least once in their lives.*

It was the biggest dream for the people of this community to pray in front of the Icon in Sumela which created miracles. The people of the region prepared for the feast on the 15th of August all year long and made all kinds of savings possible to afford the journey. For them, this visit was the longest journey that they could ever do in their lives. As the month of August approached, the pilgrimage excitement of the visitors increased. The Christians wanted to go to Sumela to pray in front of the Icon of "Virgin Mary" and witness the "Sumela Feast Service" at least once in their lives. Many Christians who lived in the Black Sea region went to Trabzon in groups by sea… Among the visitors were also the Muslims who hoped to find a cure for their illnesses. They would ask for the intercession of Virgin Mary for the healing of the illnesses of their loved ones. The Icon of "Holy Virgin" in the monastery was very famous and it was known all around the Black Sea. Both the Christian and the Muslim community respected Her and were forborne by Her. In the same period, Pontus people who lived in Russia also visited the place to visit thier relatives and participate in the feast service.

The masons, construction masters and workers would begin their work in the monastery, weeks or months before the Feast. They built shelters or lodgings, cleaned the place and around and made tents to protect people from the frequent rains and showers of the Black Sea region. All of the churches around the Monastery and in the valley below were arranged in a way to be suitable for hosting thousands of pilgrims. Especially the large area and the anterior courtyard in front of Aya Barbara Church close to the Monastery were prepared for hosting the visitors coming for the service. Lodgings and shanty structures constructed for visitors were large enough to accomodate all the villagers and the incoming tradesmen as well as their goods and animals. The dormitaries of the Monastery did not suffice for hosting thousands of people. The monks had to take precautions to accomodate those people for at least 15 days. For weeks, 15 mules of the Monastery carried flour, olives, sugar, dried beans, vegetables, fruits, salted fish and other needs from Trabzon, Maçka and Akçaabat.

The road from Trabzon to Maçka was suitable only for the passage of wheeled cars. In Maçka, the loads of the visitors were taken off, the cars were loaded on the animals; because, the road from there to the Monastery was a path that allowed only the passage of mules and passengers. The pilgrims from the villages in the valley would also join this caravan of pilgrims that set out from Trabzon. The path to Monastery could only be completed after a walk of 5 hours. When the groups of pilgrims reached the skirts of steep cliffs on which the monastery was located, they would bend on their knees and cross by looking at the sacred rocks and recited hymns. The silent and peaceful landscape would immediately take a different shape with the sounds and noises of all those men. The visitors would prepare their belongings to be on time for the morning service and would climb up the steep path to reach the Monastery on foot. When they reached the Monastery, some of them would run towards the Icon while the others put their relatives who went there for healing in front of the line. Everyone tried in a hurry to get closer to the sacred Icon to kiss Her. The visitors would eat together the food given to them by the monks after the evening service and would then resign to the places given to them for rest and sleep. It was a must that the bakery in the monastery cook breads 2-3 times a day to feed the guests.

> *"Visiting Sumela is not only a religious duty but also a matter of personal respectability. The priests and the monks that are among the candidate pilgrims overtook the duty from the*

priests and monks of the monastery and managed the services. On the 15th of August, at the end of the service held at the large church of the Monastery, the feast would begin with the music played by drums, bagpipe and fiddle. The piousness of the Black Sea people did not allow them to have a feast at the same time with the service. The end of the service would be announced with the bell of the Monastery. The feast at the end of the service would turn almost into a dancing competition. The tradesmen would sceram and sell their goods on one side while the public sat on the rugs ate, drank and sang together. The kids would play with each other and participate in this feast.

These things went on the same manner for centuries. The same preparations were carried out each year, all the people climbed up the steep cliff trying to reach "Panayia Sumela" Monastery on Mount Mela. Icon of Virgin Mary who held miracles were carried by the crowds for centuries and led everyone, from any religion, into ecstacy. The pilgrimage of the pilgrims ended when they reached the center of Trabzon." [4] (fig.9)

İsmet Zeki Eyüpoğlu narrates the presence of Sumela Monastery in the lives of the people of Maçka, thirty years after the fire in thc end of 1950s as follows:

"... Virgin Mary to whom all those who suffered, who had broken hearts ran and opened their hands to pray in hope... Virgin Mary to whom Muslims, Christians, those in pain and agony ran and bent on their knees to pray with hope. A monastery standing erect for centuries without losing anything of its character from the time that it was carved on a ledge on a considerably steep cliff twenty meters to the South of Maçka inside an evergreen forest of pinetrees and green meadows.

Nobody knows where and how the blessing came from the water that falls down from the summit of the rock in triple drops; many who are in agony and pain run for that water to drink from it and to have a bath underneath it. In Virgin Mary, the hopes are tied in small pieces of clothes and the clothes are wrapped on the stones that the water dripples on. The patches are wrapped on like this in different colours and shapes like the pains and agonies of the humankind. O, you mankind, you so many kinds of pains, wishes and hopes. It shows from the way

Figure 9- Inside main church

you go up to Virgin Mary breathlessly to pray and hope your voice to be heard.

Virgin Mary who sees the hearts and listens to the cries in silence of those coming from the plateaus around, from here and there, far away lands that most of us have not seen. The place that I came by joining the crowd of wedding ceremonies, bridal parades in the joyous days of my childhood and watched all around in amazement and astonishment my eyes wide open, my heart full of the joy of life;watching those who wished things without making any wish myself. Watching those wall size wall paintings on the destroyed hollows, the ceilings full of paintings, people with long beards in front of them murmuring prayers their arms and hands opened out to heaven. Where is Virgin Mary that was full of the joy of life that I visited at least fifty times and the full breasted beautiful girls and brides wearing the flowers of the plateau, with joyous women and children all around and the lovers flirting with their eyes? Yes, it was in ruins in the past, too, the stone and rubbles were all around the place, yet, there was something joyous, hopeful and lovely about it even in this state. Ignorant and uncivilized villagers shot bullets into the eye holes of the paintings and pulled them out of walls with the ambition of finding gold or coins hidden underneath. The so-called literate, civilized city dwellers of our time destroyed and took the wall paintings

Figure 10- The service held on the 15th of August, 2014

> *away in pieces. At Virgin Mary where illiterate and ignorant villagers and women came in hope, civilized city people chose to write down obscene wishes and funny desires. So-called literate visitors from the city wrote slang words and draw pictures and shapes as a memory (!) on the places where the illiterate public tied their wishing patches… Why, didn't Virgin Mary have enough paintings?… Thirty years ago, when Virgin Mary was burnt, even those burnt ruins had a noble and amazing look to themselves that moved the onlookers emotionally and touched their hearts."*[5]

Apart from the icon of Virgin Mary, the inscribed stavrotek (the silver cross) given as a gift to the Monastery by Manuel III had also an impact on the visitors as a valuable piece that also had a piece of the crucifix of Jesus on it. It was taken out once a month and the water was consecrated and distributed to those coming to the Monastery for healing purposes.

Moreover, both the Christians and the Muslims brought the patients to the Monastery and put them inside the cell where the water of Ayazma dropped with the expectation that they could be healed by the "sacred water" dropping on them. In his article entitled 'Public Medicine in Anatolia' the famous Author Sabahattin Eyuboğlu of Trabzon, narrates:

> *"The ill people undressed and waited for the drops to fall on their bodies. Since the drops did not always fall on the same location, a healing process of seven, ten or eleven drops would last long or short depending on the frequency of dropping. The regularity and the high frequency of the drops were considered as a sign of good luck. It is worth paying attention to the fact that Virgin Mary was considered as a source of healing in many places in Anatolia even for the Muslims. Virgin Mary might probably have substituted the place of the much earlier goddesses of Anatolia."* [6] (fig.10-11)

Since 2010, each year a service is held at the Monastery on the 15th of August, regarding the ascension of Virgin Mary according to the belief. Clergymen and the Orthodox people from Australia, Ukraine, the United States of America, Greece and Georgia participate in this service.

Figure 11- The service held on the 15th of August, 2014

INFORMATION ON THE SACRED ICON

In 1840, Fallmerayer told about in his legend the Icon and the legend of Mary, "the reason of existence" of the Monastery, with his very eyes:

"... I asked him to take us to the icon of Virgin Mary who was believed to cause miracles. Two new candles were lit and the painting was taken out of the altar. I was astonished by Saint Luke's skill and mastery of art. The turmoil of colours of the Byzantine work was made on wood in well-known style of monks. It was around a handspan in height and in an unrecognizable shape with innumerous homages paid by the Saints and, I have to say, was easily received by our art critiques as a product of the best times of Greek taste. The monks said that this was the biggest proof for the originality and the history of the work. It was made in the 17th *century by a master from Trabzon. It ornamented the sacred site of Sumela as a carved piece inside a silvery frame. You might imagine that we neither raised our suspicions about the work outloud in front of the monks nor did we dare to express a negative opinion* (fig.12).

The pious and understanding people of the solitary cave have not sufficed with blessing Kolhis and its close sorrounding with joy. They even want to offer support to the people of the regions that are the remotest to the Anatolian faith to enjoy the visit of the mystique treasures without the necessity of exerting the effort and undergoing financial burden of doing the pilgrimage. Thus, the brothers of the Monastery travel all through Asia Minor, Russia and the feudal settlements on the banks of Danube. They have rough copies of the miraculous painting in their hands and they ask for mercy and exchange the blessing of Sumela with plenty of coins. One of those monks who travelled to collect money was robbed and killed in Cappadocia a few

Figure 12- Recent apperance of icons of Mary

years before I arrived in Cesarea. The men collected 40.000 m. Turkish coins (10.000 francs) by travelling all around Anatolia begging to exchange those riches to take the money back to the sacred cave. After a hectic search, most of the stolen goods and amount were found and taken back when I was in Trabzon."[7]

Here, we need to put an end to the evaluations about the icon: In the Georgian painting art of the 12th century, some icons of Mary were known to be painted and distributed under the name of Black Madonna. In order to give her an even more mysterious look, the faces in the paintings of Virgin Mary were painted in black paint. Some icons even seemed to be blackened by means of the olive oil spread on their surfaces.

As cited by Semavi Eyice from Marie Durand-Lefebvre's *Etude sur l'origine des Vierges Noires*, although there were depictions of Mary blackened in time normally there were also Black Mary paintings that were specifically painted black which bear a separate place and importance in Art History.

The writer also stated that the paintings claimed to have been painted by Luke were suspicious and even the fact that Luke was an artist was suspicious. It was possible that Mary whose real portrait was not known could be black in colour. Yet, the following points by the writer are striking: Black Mary was mostly seen in the East of Europe, preserved especially in places of visit and on mountains inside the whorshipping places that were constructed in forests. There was also the sacred water in such places. Finally the depictions found in France were believed to have been placed where they were found miraculously.

Based on his studies in the monastery the Art historian Eyice described the above-mentioned belief regarding the foundation and the location of the icons made by Saint Luke were found as well as their impact on the people of the region (where monastery was located) and on the Orthodox believers as:

> *"It was believed that they were made when Mary and Jesus were alive and the Holy power of these two was directly reflected on the paintings. Thus, thanks to the paintings, Mary and Jesus were believed to have continued their impacts of protection, creation of miracles and healing... Some pictures were claimed to have been made by the Bible writer Luke and they were considered a proof for the production of these paintings when Jesus or Mary was alive. Thus, Mary's words "My affection and mercy come with this painting" were esteemed very highly. Worshipping a painting that was claimed to have been produced by Luke was equal to worshipping the very sacred being that the painting depicted, and thus it was believed that Her support would be received by means of this painting."* [8]

HISTORY OF THE MONASTERY

The history of the Monastery can be classified into two periods: the period before the written sources and the history that could be narrated depending on the written sources. The history of the monastery dates back to the 4th century in 386 according to the legend created before the written sources. This legend is still being told by the society of the Monastery and the Orthodox community and it was actually written by Fotiadis[9]. When we take the records of Prokopius into consideration, in contradiction with the other sources, the originating date was taken as the Era of Justinianus[10]. As stated by Fallmerayer, even if we wanted to write the history of the Monastery by taking the reliable sources such as these as the basis of our information, we should not ignore the following statement by the author above: "*... without looking at its previously strong outlook, the structure frequently fell victim to the enemy forces and was burnt down and deserted for generations...*" It is for sure that there are periods before the beginning of the reliable records of history that must be taken into account in terms of the past of the monastery. This is not a period of history to be told with confidence. Of course, there are accounts that can be named as historical starting with the "journey of the sacred icon in the hands of the angels" and the period that started as the history of the Skhamalinihi Church that lasted until the era of Komnenos dynasty. Yet, there is no written source in our hand today about those periods. The sentence in the Trabzon Travelogue of Prokopius referring to this information may be taken seriously as a possibility since it was written by a historian as an evaluation.

The legend of founding told in history according to written sources narrates that the two priests from Athens, Barnabas and Sophronios, established the place at the time of Theodosios and Belisarios. A commander of Justinianos had it subsequently restored. However, as stated above, this story of founding was not based on a strong evidential source. If we leave this legend aside, it is possible for us to read the history of the monastery today at least from 13th century onwards. Sumela Monastery took its place in history with that name, only at the time of Komnenos principality in Trabzon. Komnenos Principality of Trabzon was born out of the Byzantine Empire as a separate state and started to develop as such. It ruled the region having Trabzon as the capital city. Trabzon Princes showed their state as the legal heir of the Byzantine Empire and presented themselves as Emperors. This title was not recognized by the real Byzantine Empire which reclaimed Istanbul in 1261 and made the old Byzantine state flourish. Alexios III of the Komnenos of Trabzon having their own political strategies and close and intricate relationship especially with the Turkish principalities may be considered as the real founders of this monastery. The sources and documents show that Alexios III, two of whose sisters were married with Turkish beys and who gave his four daughters as brides to the neighbouring Turkish beys, esteemed Sumela very highly. Since it is also known that his grand grand father, grand father and father made donations for the monk cells of the monastery, it can be said that there was a religious center there since the time of Alexios' grand grand father Ioannes II(1280-1285). According to another legend survived until today, Alexios III who was saved during a major storm since Mary had the premises constructed all over again as a complex of structures and donated foundations to it, and then by an edict (khrisoboullos) he arranged strong legal grounds for these foundational rights. The inscription of five lines in verse form dated 1360 that could be seen on the outer gate of the monastery since 1650, said that Alexios III was the founder (kretor) of the building as the "Sovereign Emperor of the East and West (=Iberia)". Alexios welcomed the solar eclipse of 1361 there. The depiction of the sun on the coins of the prince was accepted to be a symbol of the event. In accordance with the "act of foundation" (vakfiye) dating to 1364, all of the administrational conditions, land and income of the monastery were rearranged and the monks were warned to remain vigilant at all times as a precaution againt a possible threat of a Turkish attack to Trabzon. This edict (khrisoboullos) by Aleksios III dating to 1364 was recorded in the artefacts inventory of Hagia Sofia (Ayasofya) Museum as in item no. 12901. The width of this edict written on paper with black ink was 30 cm. and its length was 335 cm. Its text took 100 lines. The text of the edict is as follows:

1. This Monastery shall be independent and free in the future and it shall only be ruled by Emperor Aleksios Komnenos III without any support and of help of anyone.

2. The land and assets of the Monastery which were gained according to the edicts or as a gift of the previous emperors or by means of the wills of the pieous people who loved Jesus Christ or by way of purchase shall never be taken from the Monastery.

3. The inheritance of land and the assets of the inhabitants including both those who live in the farms owned by the monastery and those who officially reside and work in the monastery shall be directly left to the monastery in case of their death without leaving a heir.

4. The water mills, work places, real estate, land and buildings given by Aleksios Komnenos and other people to the monastery as gifts shall always remain to be the propriety of the monastery.

5. The observation tower at the top of the monastery shall defend the monastery against a possible threat from the neighbouring Turkish beys with the selected best equipped and most vigilant soldiers.

Son of Alexios, Manuel III (1390-1417) was a person adhering to the religious premises like his father. The year he was enthroned, he gave a precious stavrotek from the palace treasury (the silver cross that is claimed to have a piece of thc crucifix of Christ in it) as a gift to Sumela. The last Komnenos of Trabzon made Sumela monastery richer with their edicts or certified their foundations.

Following the conquest of Trabzon and its environs by the Turks, the Ottoman Sultans meticulously preserved the previous status and legal rights of the monastery as they did in Aynaroz, Sina and many other monasteries, and they even issued privileges and sent certain gifts to the monastery. Likewise, the two candle holders in Sumela, were known to have been given by Sultan Selim (1512-1520) as a gift. An edict issued by Sultan Mehmet, the conqueror of Trabzon, ruled that the legal rights of the monastery were recognized and reserved by him directly. Other sources on the monastery tell us about the existence of other edicts safeguarding the above-mentioned rights. There were also similar edicts known to have been issued by the Sultans Beyazıt II, Selim I, Selim II, Murad III, Ibrahim, Mehmet IV, Suleiman II, Mustafa and Ahmet III.

As from the second half of the 18th century, the voivodes of Wallachia were interested in the monastery and therefore, continously sent donations and written documents to it.

Sumela was especially developed in the 18th century under the guardianship of the voivodes and many of its parts were restored. In 1749, an Archbishop named Ignatios had all the façades of the walls ornamented with frescos. Sumela had its golden age in the 19th century with the unprecedented vigorous organisation and enrichment of all of the Greek-Orthodox communities in Anatolia, and the churches and monasteries were accordingly restored and ornamented magnificently with the help of the money donated by external sources. German historian Fallmerayer visiting the monastery as a guest has perused and analyzed the documents as regards the history of Trabzon which were full of the complaints of the monks who lived in the monastery. In their complaints, the monks asserted that they were only after their interests and remained ignorant to scientific developments. He said the following words in the Turkish language, to the monk who stood by his side in an annoyed manner as he was analyzing the magnificent gilded edict with miniatures of Alexios III and his wife on it (golden seals missing):

> *"Karabaş (monk in old language) what do you mean, is your mind inside your brains (a saying that means, are you out of your mind), this thing would yield both bread and would be esteemed in Western neighbourhoods (countries)!" This showed*

both the indifference and the ignorance of the monks as well as proving that they spoke Turkish not Greek.

Likewise, the same historian gives the book on the creed of Christianity published by the voivode of Wallachia Skarlatos Ghikas in 1768 in Bucharest as an example for the fact that the monks used to speak Turkish only. The book was translated into Turkish, as the only language spoken in the monastery and was published in the Greek alphabet by Parthenios Metaxopoulos, a spiritual figure and a member of Sumela Monastery. The book in question also included a chapter on the founding legend of Sumela Monastery entitled "a good account of Sumela Panagia Monastery of the Esteemed Sultan and Bishop"(Azim Padişahlık ve Patriklik Sumela Panagia'nın Manastırı için güzel nakliet). It also included a Hymn in verse form written for Mary of Sumela in Turkish with the Greek letters. As mentioned above and put forth by Fallmerayer in 1840, the travelling monks of Sumela travelled all around Anatolia, Caucasus, Balkans and even Russia to collect money by selling a bad copy of the icon of Mary and brought the money back to their organisations. The facility became richer in the 19th century and towards the year 1860, it turned into a fully-fledged complex of buildings with the construction of the structures that may be observed on the façade. In the 19th century, Sumela was visited by many travellers. Those travellers generously shaped their observations during the visits. Some parts from those observations are given below.

Colonel Rottiers who returned in 1818 to his homeland from Tiblisi after long years of service for Russians stayed in Trabzon for a while. He recorded that he had his lunch his way to Gümüşhane at Prodromos Monastery and spent the night at Virgin Mary Monastery; that the monks were hospitable and a portrait of Mary found there attracted crowds of visitors each year. Another foreigner visiting Sumela was E. Zacharia. The facility that he saw on July 24th, 1838 was a monastery which was very hard to climb at that time and one could only reach its gate of entrance by wooden skeletons by means of the suspended bridges that were released for the visitors only. The monastery had a strong iron gate but looked poor with only twenty-thirty monks residing in it. According to the account of Tozer, the roof of the chapel in front of the hollow that seemed to be protruded was covered in copper.

According to the accounts by the Armenian geographers (cf. Ritter, Erdkunde-Kleinasien, p. 911) the copper roof mentioned above was made upon the order of Sultan Murad IV. The monks of the monastery made a strange story out of this generous gesture to tell foreign visitors. According to the story Sultan Murad wanted to bombard the monastery, yet, when the cannon balls did not fire, he came to appreciate the grandeur of Virgin Mary (!) and he promised to cover the roof in silver on his way from Baghdad. Yet, he kept his promise by covering it only in copper! This cannot be true at all. The old cannon balls could not fire from ground to air. This insulting story was also told not for Murad but for Sultan Selim. With respect to this rumour, there is also certain information provided by Minas Bijishkyan from Trabzon in his travel notes on the Black Sea coasts (1817-1819):

> *"Virgin Mary is a famous Greek monastery above Hoşoğlan, between Trabzon and Gümüşhane. This old building constructed on the edge of the mountain slopes inside the rocks may only be ascended by means of very narrow stairs folded up after use in order to be protected from the bandits. The*

church of the monastery is a considerably respected place of visit. The Muslims also visit it and send candles. The two long and thick candles in the church looking like posts are said to be donated by Sultan Murad. Rumour has it that the Sultan was passing through there and promised to cover the church in gold if he was victorious in his Baghdad expedition, but the monks wanted to have it covered in lead and eventually the Sultan sent those giant candles to them". (fig.13)

In the second half of the 19th century, British travellers H. F. Tozer and M. P. Warkworth visited the monastery and provided short but useful information about the place. G. Palgrave (1826-1888) was one of those who provided the most detailed information on the monastery in one of his articles entitled "the monastery of Sumelas" published first in Fraser's Magazine and then in his book published in February 1871 with the other articles. The writer stated that the legend that Sultan Murat had the monastery fired with cannons as he passed there was not possible. When Palgrave reached there the big building seen from the façade then called "the new building"-was finished only three years ago. According to the observations of this British writer, the structure had seven floors including the arches on the precipice, and its real area of settlement had four rows of windows with also a gallery on top of it.

There were eight rooms on each storey stretching a long line identically and in general it appeared to be a very strong building. Palgrave also mentioned that he saw the gifts by Murad and Selim I as well as the edict of Alexios III with a miniature. Palgrave saw an edict by Selim II and he openly said that he did not like the monks' speaking against Sultan Selim II.

German officer E. von Hoffmeister visited the monastery in the beginning of the 20th century, and published in

Figure 13- Sumela Monastery on the Karadağ was built clinging to a cliff face

his book a beautiful overview of the monastery from a distance. He also published a good picture of the pictoresque houses with wooden patios (the traces of which cannot be found anywhere today) that were lined on the left of the stairs. The writer stated that the icon of Virgin Mary was in a miserable state and added in rejection of the lies alleging that the Turks were trying to destroy the monastery and that the fifteen monks who lived in that big monastery at the time were liars. They tried insistently to show the foreigners how poor they were so that they could receive donations.

In brief, it seems that the majority of the foreign travellers visiting Sumela Monastery admired the natural beauty of the place, but did not have a very positive impression of its community.

THE DOWNFALL OF THE MONASTERY AND THE SACRED RELICS

As a result of the population exchange in 1923 following the signing of the Armistice of Maudros, the monks had to leave the monastery with the impact of the activities initiated in the region for the purpose of establishing a Pontus Greek Republic. Then, the religious activities of the monastery ended upon the monks' leaving the place. Before the monks left the monastery, they burried the sacred relics of the monastery in front of the small church which is situated at a distance of around 1 km. which was built by Saint Sofronios in the name of Saint Barnabas.

Among those relics were the Sumela icon made by Saint Luke which accounted for the global reputation of the monastery, the manuscript of the Bible copied on a parchment paper by Saint Christopher and the holy cross (stavrotek) given by Emperor Manuel Komnenos as a gift.

The monastery had a ruinous appearance with all the rubbles in it after the fire of 1929 and the indifference and lack of maintenance in the years that followed the fire, not to mention the destruction that the bandists seeking for treasures have caused.

On August 15, 1931, a religious service and celebration was held at Megalo Spileoda Panagia Church in Kalavryta. The service was joined by the Prime Minister of Greece of the time, Venizelos and a community, the majority of which were Pontus Greeks. At the end of the ceremony, the bishop of Xanti (Gümülcine) Polycarpos

Psomiades who served as the army bishop in Anatolia, told the Greek Prime Minister Venizelos the story of where and how the icon painted by Saint Luke, was burried in the Black Sea region.

When Prime Minister of Turkey, Ismet Inonu visited Athens for the Balkan Olympic Games in September 1931, Venizelos asked for Inonu's permission to release the icon from the place it was buried (in the grave of a monk). Venizelos assigned bishop Hrisantos and Hrisantoschoe, a priest named Ambrossios to fulfill this task. They went to Agia Barbara chapel in Trabzon escorted by the police and the soldiers to find the buried icon and other relics to take them to the Byzantine Museum in Athens. The pieces brought from Sumela were preserved for 20 years in the Benaki Museum in Athens.

In 1950, Dr. Philon Ktenidesa, a Greek with Black Sea origin, launched a campaign among the Greeks with Black Sea origin in order to place the miraculous Sumela icon painted by Saint Luke in a monastery and also to construct a monastery similar to the Sumela Monastery in Trabzon.

As a result of that campaign, on August 15, 1952, the new monastery constructed in Veriya on Vermion Mountain was named the Sumela Monastery and the Sumela Icon preserved in Benaki Museum for 20 years was placed in that new monastery, as well.

SETTLEMENT AND ARCHITECTURAL FEATURES

The monasteries were developed as a part of seclusion in Budism, Hinduism and Christianity. The monks undergoing an ordeal and agony spent their lives in the monasteries by praying for the religion that they worshipped by secluding themselves from all the riches and comforts of the world as a self-accepted requirement of their worship and belief.

Selection of the location for the construction of a monastery is very important. Monasteries were always built in places far from the crowded areas of settlement, particularly on routes that were difficult to access. The large hollows in the rocks on isolated locations and the ledges of the steep and massive rocks overlooking the valley that may be accessed only through high and inclined paths were such places. Another reason for that choice was that Mary gave birth to Jesus inside a cave and the caves became the natural locations of the monasteries built in the name of Mary.

Sometimes, the priests and the nuns lived together in the monastery and ruled the monastery together. Sumela is a monastery for men only. The exiled princes, rebels from the dynasties and the clergy men were imprisoned in monasteries to receive training to persuade them to leave their opponent ideas and activities. Likewise, Eyüpoğlu has the following record in his book: *"The documents state that some of the convicts who were sent from Istanbul in the beginning of the 19th century, were imprisoned in the Virgin Mary Monastery* *by an edict of the Sultan who survived our time"*[11] Virgin Mary Monastery was important even in those ages for different reasons.

The biggest source of income of the monasteries was the donations, and the taxes that they collected from the villages in the area which were part of their foundation. The donations were collected by the monks who devoted their lives to the monastery. The monks especially those residing in the Eastern Orthodox Christianity served the monastery just like the Anatolian dervishes served with the philosophy of "a cloak and a morsel". As of the beginning of the 13th century, the monasteries lost their financial power and importance with the downfall of feudalism in Western Europe and the questioning of the power of the church. Despite that fact, they preserved their power and influence in Eastern Christianity until the beginning of the 19th century mainly because the Ottoman Empire ruled in the regions in question at the time and did not interfere with the life in the monasteries (fig.14).

The view of the complex in the Sumela Monastery which evolved in time is as follows (fig.15):

General View

The entrance of the monastery, located on the south of Altındere Valley like a lump of a white mark on the eastern wall of the dark massive rock inside the green landscape, was controlled very strictly. It could only be accessed at the end of climbing up by a narrow and long stairs of 64 steps. Roman style large aqueduct next to the stairs that recline on the slope shows that water was brought to the monastery in the past, from a distance of about 4 km. i.e. from the skirts of Karaağaç Plateau.

Figure 14- Fresco on the Wall at forbidden area

Figure 15- 64 Stepping staircase to entrance

Figure 16- Roman style large aqueduct next to the stairs

The aqueduct seen in the old pictures perfectly with its large curve and ten holes was destroyed in time because of the rocks falling from above. Yet, it reclaimed the old form with a restoration (fig.16-17).

There is a small inner courtyard that may be accessed after passing through the door and the cells of the guards that may be descended with 92 steps. At this point, the view of the monastery is not as attractive as it is seen from outside. Everything is about 15 m. down and looks small because of the impact of the gigantic rock. As you begin to descend, the structures become bigger and may thus be better perceived. On the way down the right of the stairs are the library and personnel rooms placed at different layers. The courtyard on the ground is the center of the settlement. Around the courtyard across from the descending stairs are several small chapels. In the old photographs of the monastery taken before, it received its current form with wooden balconies and porches on top of one another on the façade of all the buildings that overlooked the courtyard.

Figure 17- Entrance door

As stated by Talbot-Rice, there were beautiful objects on them carved on wood. Paintings estimated to date to 14th or 15th century were found in one of the small chapels which is under restoration today.

Structures Situated on the right of the Courtyard

To the right of the courtyard, when we take the descending stairs to our back is the big building used as a dormitory and guest house that is known to date to the middle of the 19th century and claimed to have had 72 rooms before the fire. The building is located in a narrow corridor on a narrow overhang in front of the rock (fig.18). It is a grand building that directly leans on the slope. This part that is always in the foreground in the pictures of Sumela Monastery from a distance is the main monastery structure which was used by the monks as lodging. This section is a structure with a height of 17 m. and a length of 40 m. long and a width of 14 m. The stones needed for the construction of the building were suitable for processing and were brought from the Santa plateaus 17 km. far from there.

Apart from the three main storeys, this structure which appeared to have a cellar of several rows below and an additional floor at the top had a magnificent and majestic appearance with the vaulted galleries lined up at the bottom of the eaves. This building with the structure of a lodging, resembling a white mark from a distance as if overhanging from the rocks of the mountain, was constructed during the major activity of restoring and expanding the monastery in 1860. It is a building which has no architectural significance apart from a giant size. Its wooden roof which used to have wide eaves, the interior sections and the wooden storeys are in the process of restoration. Looking from

Figure 18- The building is located in a narrow corridor on a narrow overhang in front of the rock

Figure 19- Room

the middle tower that creates a downward overhanging form, one sees the dizzying height and horrendousness of the building.

The section seen on the right while passing through the entrance door and descending the inner stairs is the four storey area where the bedrooms, living halls, library, cellar, toilets and the eating areas are found. In all rooms are furnaces, light closets and surfaces for keeping the books (fig.19). The rooms and exedra (eyvan)have balconies overhanging towards the inner façade. The balconies currently undergo restoration and wait for a reconstruction (fig.20). At the very bottom are a kitchen with a vault and the areas used for preserving the wine and oil underneath it. All of the walls are attached to one another with intermingling linear beams made of elm tree and oak. The thickness of the walls varies from approximately 60 cm. to 100 cm. The windows are made of carved stone and do not

Figure 20- Stock room

have any arches. There are no paintings on the walls. This section of Virgin Mary was placed on four arches that are opened in the front like a door. The foundation of the wall was set on the rock top to bottom beginning with the acute-angled side of the triangular form. This section displays the impact of medieval aspect in terms of the structural form, too. The thing that is worth discussing in terms of architectural structure is its medieval aspects. We do not know the real number of the rooms today since they were destroyed. Yet, when we look at the foundational structure of the building, the number of the rooms ranges from 20 to 30. The entrances of the rooms face the courtyard. Generally, there is a furnace right across the entrance and windows on both sides of the furnace overlooking the valley and niches and closets on the side walls. The windows and doors have cut stone beams and arches (fig.21).

The niches and closets buried into the walls and displayed the impact of the architecture of the region.

Figure 21- Room

The ceilings and the floorings of the rooms of the monastery which are close to a square in form are wooden. The door and window cavities are small and the walls are thick. The reason for this is to have the least impact of the hard climatic conditions. As a result of the major restorations carried out on the monastery building, the rooms and the levels are now visible.

This part was known to have been constructed in three phases. Firstly, the chambers of the monks located in the northern part (1860) were constructed. Then, the section in the south stretching to the library (1886-1903) was constructed. After that, the building of the monastery was raised in 1903 with another layer, and additional structures such as chimneys and niches were built in the interior sections. Both the rooms and the other sections clearly display the construction technique and the lay-out of the Medieval Age. This can be easily told by the masonry and patterns of the walls. This section of Virgin Mary is set on the rock firmly giving all the weight to the east of the rock. The variety of stones used in this section is soft in kind and it is difficult to work on accordingly.

Structures Situated on the Left of the Courtyard (fig.22)

The church on the left of the courtyard embellished with frescos is the center of the premise. The place where the church, as the oldest structure of the settlement, is situated, is in a natural hollow. On the right and left of the church covering an area of 400 square meters, we see the Ana Kaya (Main Rock) Church, also called as Mağara (Cave) Church, and several buildings established without a certain plan exist, as well.

Both the inner walls and the outer wall (visible from outside) of the church built next to the chapel lapping towards the courtyard are all covered with the fresco paintings. Yet, when you look closer and analyze them, most of these paintings date to a later time made on top of the older and more valuable wall paintings in the sub layers. This was already mentioned by other researchers (fig 23).

Figure 22- Left side of complex

Next to the church, on the left where the triple drops fall down from the rock is a sacred water source (ayazma). It can be said to have been built later in time because of the close similarity of its stone ornamentations to the works in Anatolian Seljuk style.

On the north of the worshipping area are three or four cells, the walls and ceilings of which are painted. The paintings on these sections are assumed to have been built at later ages as it may be seen by the workmanship and the paint that is used. On the south of "ayazma" (on the left) is a furnace with a small cellar next to it. Part of the furnace is flat while the other parts are made of hollow bricks. The holes of the bricks tell us that this section was restored later since the hollow brick material was used in recent ages.

Figure 23- Left side of center

Façades

Sumela Monastery has two façades. One is the façade of the monastery building and other structures facing the courtyard, and the other one is the façade that overlooks the valley (fig 24). When the wall of the monastery overlooking the courtyard is analyzed, the traces of the wooden stairs and balconies serving as a passage among the rooms and storeys can be seen.

The wooden galleries serving as a passage way, that were built on the wooden posts and burnt down in the fire, create a dynamic structure in the courtyard façade. On the façade where the monks' rooms overlook the courtyard, the doors with the stone beams and the traditionally constructed stone beams of the windows are seen (fig 25).

The (eastern) façade overlooking the valley is the main façade of the monastery building. What we know about it is that it is the façade that is seen on the cliff

Figure 24- Inner, western façade of the monastery

in the north-south direction as if wrapping the cliff and making the grandeur of the monastery visible to the eyes. The monastery is generally known by this façade. The graded plan of the building from the entrance is better appreciated from this façade, too (fig 26). The open exedra located in the middle of the area where the rooms of the monks are found continues for four floors by giving the façade an air of dynamism with its columns and vaults. The vaulted column structure below the wide eaves of the roof decreases the heavy look of the building. On this façade are the windows constructed in the same proportions and framed with stone beams (fig.27).

Eastern section of the monastery is light, spacious and high with a wide span of view. The hollow of the western section of the church is closed, dark, compressed, gloomy and heavy in atmosphere since it is inside the cave. Looking at it from inside, the section where the church is located is buried inside the rock, the building where the rooms are located, on the other hand, looks like a patch on the rock. This shows us that the two sections were constructed during two different periods by different people.

It is apparent that Virgin Mary was constructed, restored and expanded with certain additions in phases at different ages whether by looking at the section where the Cave Church is located or by looking at the other sections. The width of the area that it covered in terms of its availability for expansions and its reputation urged it to expand with certain additions in a short period of time. The crown ceremony of a Pontus King is enough to prove the importance that it was given. Many important visitors that it received afterwards, made

Figure 25- Known façade, east side of monastery

Figure 26- The open exedra

Virgin Mary even more esteemed. The construction of the second section in a more attractive manner and in a way to provide more convenient living conditions is a sign of the use of the monastery for very important purposes.

The water was brought to the monastery from the Santa plateaus in the west by means of the arches in old Roman style inside brick pipes (fig.28). There were water ducts made of stone inside the structure that collected the falling rain. Today, only the vague traces of all of those are left. Inside Virgin Mary Monastery, there were also the sections in the lowest floor that were used for the storage of the materials used in the church as well as a prison for the convicts and the detention rooms used for punishment. There are documents that reached our time stating that in the beginning of the 19th century, some convicts sent from Istanbul were imprisoned in Virgin Mary Monastery with the edict of the Sultan. İsmet Zeki Eyüpoğlu has the following

Figure 27- Inside exedra

account in his book: *"On the façade that overlooked the stream, those who would be executed were thrown from a dark hole below. Bones and gold rings of many dead people were found there until recently. The father of the writer of these lines also found such rings. Below the rock by the stream were found many of such human remains."*

Figure 28- Brick pipes

LIBRARY

Fallmerayer states having seen, during this visit, the books that were piled inside a cave with no light (fig.29). Nothing important could be found inside the cave library which can only be descended by means of stairs, where there used to be books published in Europe. Papadopoulos-Keramevs prepared a catalogue of the manuscripts there and the other researchers added a few more manuscripts to the list. These manuscripts that were 85-90 in number were scattered after the monastery was evacuated. One of those, the Bible that was copied by Saint Christopher on a parchment paper is now being exhibited in the Byzantine Museum in Athens, while the majority is currently kept in Ankara. Some of the documents and papers owned by the monastery, were scattered in the

Figure 29- Library

market while some were taken to Greece. Most of the manuscripts preserved in Ankara corresponded to a time after the 17th century. Among these, though, there are also three separate sets of four Bibles (Tetraevangelium) dating to the 11th and 12th centuries. Although it is clear that these were gilded and had miniatures, they were in a ruinous shape. Among the religious books of the 17th and 18th centuries were the 2 Akoluthia of Saint Barnabas and Sophronios.

One of the two manuscripts on Profan is the chronographies of Byzantine Emperors and Ottoman Sultans written by Manuel Malaxos in the end of the 16th century. The other one is the list of the Christian inhabitants of the city of Sinop prepared in 1691 by Khristophoros, son of Stephanos. Among the manuscripts in Ankara are also the books of letters, protocol and expenses of the monastery that belonged to the 18th and 19th centuries. There certainly are some other documents and books in the market and in the private collections. Likewise, a little while ago in Istanbul some documents with the appropriation seal of the monastery were seen to be on sale. A copy of the four Bibles (Tetraevangelium) with valuable miniatures in it is said to be transferred to the Archaeology Museum in Istanbul. Some documents about Sumela Monastery are currently found in Athens as well as the two church objects with Sumela Monastery origin which are currently in the Benaki Museum of Athens. One of these objects is a silver medallion that depicted the Christian trinity (Teslis) and the other one is an epitaphios, a cover with embellishments with the script of the foundation on it dating to 1438.

AYAZMA

One of the factors that made Virgin Mary so sacred and famous was its sacred water resource (ayazma) (fig.30). There is no other water resource in the Maçka region or in the Black Sea Region or maybe even in the world with triple drops coming down from such a high and stiff rock.The triple drop of the water coming from inside the peak of the rock is the aspect of the water that can easily be associated with the Christian belief. The similarity between the holy trinity (father-son-holy spirit) of the Christian religion and that water makes it easier to attribute sacredness to the water. When this parallelism is added to the sacredness of water and the belief that is found in almost all religions about the secret and sacred powers of the water, the sacredness of the Virgin Mary Monastery, needs no further explanation.

Figure 30- Ayazma

The belief that the dripping water had a healing power and that undressing the hopelessly ill people and counting the number of healing drops hitting any part of their bodies (seven, eleven or twenty one drops) renders the Monastery important for the believers of different religions. There are sacred water sources called "ayazma"in many esteemed places. This sacredness is in parallel with the attribution of Virgin Mary as a "spring of vital source". These waters are believed to save the guilty off their guilt, those in agony off their agony and those in pain off their pains. The believers go into those waters to take a bath and get cleansed. Such waters are accepted as sacred in the religions of old Anatolia, India, China, Iran, Sumer, Kaide and Egypt. This is true for the religions in Rome, Phonenicia and Greece. This old belief had important impacts on Christianity and Islam. The old religions apparently had an important impact on the attribute of sacredness of Virgin Mary.

Virgin Mary is a site which is esteemed as a sacred place by the believers of almost all religions (except for the Jews). It owes this quickly disseminating fame to its power of opening its doors to all who are in pain and agony.

The impact of the Turkish art is occasionally seen on the buildings around the courtyard. The fountain collecting the sacred water also reflected the Turkish architectural style with its conic arches. The most interesting point though was the wall ornamentations on some of the walls made in dark red paint. These ornamentations are the copies of the brick grouting ornamentations of the 18th century Turkish buildings with "ayazma" structure in the form of painting.

SURROUNDING BUILDINGS

Before the entrance gate of the monastery, from the point where the vehicles are left onwards, there are two more structures that can be seen at the end of the road that led to the right. The first one of these is the small church that is named Ayavarvara located on a rock. Women resided in the buildings next to it and they took care of the cows of the monastery as

Figure 31- Ayavarvara

Figure 32- Ayavarvara

well as doing the other chores. The women could not go into the monastery to worship as mixed with the men. This was a vaulted small building. It had sleeping areas, soup kitchen and lodgings. It was built a while after the construction of the monastery. It stood right across from Virgin Mary and also had a secure entrance gate (fig.31-32).

The building located right across from the entrance gate of the monastery is the stable where the animals that carried the food and other materials were kept. This building currently serves as a cafeteria.The water of the fountain next to the cafeteria is cold enough even in

Figure 33- Byre, cafeteria

August to refresh the visitors who enjoyed and admired it (fig.33).

The places where those who took care of the gardens, woods and forests of the monastery were also located outside the monastery.

Virgin Mary Monastery had a variety of large fields land, meadows, gardens, forests, houses that supported the financing, shopping places, cattle, sheep, horses and mules. It was almost the most sacred and rich area of Pontus. It had plenty of carpets, rugs, ornamentations, paintings carved on wood. The food was prepared in large boilers and numerous guests were hosted there.

RESTORATION AND CLEANING ACTIVITIES

The work that served for the maintenance and restoration of the destroyed parts of the monastery was initiated in 1962 with the repair of the stairs and the gate. In 1972, at the end of the restoration work that was carried out with intervals, as from 1967, the site was opened for visits as a historical site. In 1981, the monastery was given the status of a natural site and in 1987 it was taken under conservation with the declaration of Altındere Valley as a National Park. Ten years after that (1997), the monastery area was declared as a natural and archaeological site of 1st degree of importance by the Trabzon Council for the Conservation of Cultural and Natural Assets while its surroundings were declared as a site of 2nd degree of importance (fig.34).

The Turkish Ministry of Culture and Tourism launched the work of restoration in order for Sumela Monastery to be included into the Provisional List of "World Heritage". The Ministry stated that the monastery was in UNESCO World Heritage Sites. The restoration projects planned to be undertaken with interdisciplinary and integrative approach would be initiated after the assessment of the current status of the monastery with the land measurements and documentation of its condition were completed.

The conservation of the frescos on the walls of Sumela was stated to be undertaken by Istanbul Directorate of Central and Regional Restoration and Conservation Laboratories of the Ministry of Culture and Tourism.

The project was stated to undertake the building survey, restitution and restoration work in three phases. It was added that the project had a world wide importance in terms of its design, materials, architecture and workmanship.

The construction technique of Sumela Monastery displays a characteristic of simple piling technique. Stone, wood, sand from the streams and limestone were used as construction materials and the details were given by means of traditional construction techniques. On all of the walls of the building the stone materials brought from the stone mines in the area were used. The coating material of the interiors was made of water with hay mixture and limestone and then whitewashed outside.

The historical research and explorations show that the structure basically had two materials. These materials are wood and stone, which were widespreadly used in the architecture of the region. Two different types of stone materials were used in the construction. All of the load bearing walls of the monastery were made of arches while the garden walls and the pavement stones of the courtyard, though limited in space, were made of broken stones. The carved and cut stones were in general made of fine carving and cut stone techniques were used in the vaults, steps, interior and exterior flooring, furnaces, niches, windows and door beams of the monastery. The wooden materials were taken from the hard trees such as chestnut and hornbeam that were widely used in the region. The blackpine which is peculiar to the region was used on the ceiling and floor woodworks.

Sumela Monastery can not be said to display a high architectural quality but it is important for its location.

Figure 34- Karadağ and the Monastery

Such structures and settlements built on rocks, can be found in a limited range of areas. Thinking about the time and the technology of their construction, it is especially important that such structures may be built. Since this complex of structures had units with different space constructions as it was built in different periods, the projects of restoration and restitution were also undertaken in phases. These phases can be listed as follows: The arrangement of the aqueducts and the first courtyard; the project that covered the entrance tower, the control building and the library buildings; the restoration project of the lodgings of the monks and living area; the restoration of the area used by the archbishop and seclusion areas and the arrangement of the inner courtyard.

In the restorations undertaken to date, different restoration techniques were applied because of the architectural and spatial characteristics of the monastery.

Improving: This technique was applied in simple operations most of the time. The missing elements of the structure or the parts in bad shape were partially restored. This was especially applied partially on the stairs, the flooring of the courtyard and the window and door beams. The missing or damaged stones of the steps were replaced with the new ones. Likewise, the stone flooring of the courtyard was improved and dark brown carved stone copings were put on the stone walls in the courtyard. The parts around the courtyard that look ruined or about to collapse, were also fortified.

Completing and Reconstructing: The parts that collapsed or destroyed all together in time were completed in accordance with the visual and written documents. The most interesting work of completion was carried out in the section of the monastery where the rooms of the monks were located and some areas around the courtyard (kitchen and chapel walls).The kitchen found in the courtyard was completed. The sacred water area (ayazma), other areas and incomplete parts of the walls were also completed and they gained a totally new look in the end. The wall on the side of stairs leading down into the courtyard and the copings on it as well as the terrace walls were totally renewed. Especially the kitchen and the ayazma structure next to it almost gained the appearance of a brand new building after the restoration. This significant change was a result of the selection of appropriate materials, workmanship and the reconstruction of the structures which looked ruinous before the restoration.

Looking at the pictures of the section on the right where the rooms of the monks were located before the big fire in 1929, we see a traditional wood coated stopped roof with wide eaves. Setting out from this background information, the old walls that looked totally ruinous were completed and the buliding took its final form with the construction of a roof that looked like the old roof coating. Thus, the roofless building where the ruinous walls embracing the cliff were foregrounded (when looked at it from the valley before the restoration), was now perceived as a totally new structure with its modular, wide eaved and brick covered roof structure. The purpose of the completion technique applied to the roofs was to bring the historical identity of the building back. The completion of the floorings in the same section helped the rooms of the monastery to be percieved in a better way. The furnaces found in the rooms, the niches, door and window beams were replaced with the new cut stone materials.

Cleaning: It was specifically applied on the frescos inside and outside the church and on some surfaces. The cleaning of the frescos that were damaged in the fire was carried out in different phases and times.

Freezing: In the first periods of the application phase of the restoration project, the completion and renewal operations were carried out on some of the ruins and wall remains in the courtyard. Yet, some parts were left as they were due to the significant change in the outlook that came as a result of this operation. It made the restored parts look as if they were built anew while the other parts in question were left as they were. So, for those parts, the method of preserving the forms as they were (without applying any operation), was preferred.

Sumela Monastery which is one of the most important cultural assets in the world and in our country due to its historical importance requires a serious restorational operation. This structure which symbolizes the faith and the zeal of mankind from the history to our day will survive for many more years and will continue to be an important touristic center in that region.

LEGENDS OF THE MONASTERY

The exact age and date of the construction of the monastery and those who constructed it were not known for sure. Furthermore, considering the beauty of its location in all respects including the trees and the water source; the mankind took the chance of using his imagination the way he liked. He created several unrealistic stories about Virgin Mary Monastery and also found the historical justifications for these stories to prove their truth and authenticity. The purpose was to claim and announce the sacredness of what was offered to them as a blessing and accordingly they did their best to serve that purpose.

Here is what has been told about the monastery in a story:

Sultan Murad IV launched two expeditions to the East. These were known in history as Baghdad and Revan expeditions (1622-1639). As he was returning from the Revan Expedition, the Sultan passed through the high hills of the Yazlık Village over Maçka which was across from the Virgin Mary Monastery. The Sultan looked up when he reached Seslikaya right across from Virgin Mary; saw the Monastery and ordered his men to bombard it.When he could not achieve it he came to realize the sacredness of the place and sent the monks living there, coins and gold. This can not be true at all. The old balls could not bombard from top to bottom, so this story was nothing more than a coinage. Moreover, the Ottoman Sultans were never known to have bombarded and pulled down the monasteries.

It would be enough for Sultan Murad to send a few people to take over the Monastery he did not have to pull it down all thogether.

Another story that was told with reference to Sultan Murat and also to Sultan Mehmed the Conqueror (i.e.the Conqueror of Trabzon):

There is this good tasting water that people of Maçka drink today which comes from the Yazlık Village. This water is called "Sultan Murad's Water". Sultan Murad felt very tired and thirsty on the road and when they arrived at the Yazlık Village he sat by the source of that water and asked for some water from a beautiful Greek girl who was filling her buckets from the spring. The girl filled in the container and took the water to the Sultan but spilt it on the ground before giving it to him. She did it for a few times and then gave the Sultan the water. The Sultan drank it up and then asked the girl why she gave it to him after having spilt for a few times. The girl answered him by saying: "*My Sultan, you were tired and this water makes those who drink it when they are tired sick indeed. It is very good for those who are restful, that is why I tried to keep you busy for a while until you got rid of your tiredness*". Then, the Sultan liked the girl and married her.

Here is the legend still being told by the Christians:

> *The icon described above which was very highly esteemed and accepted as a source of healing for Christians was kept in the Sumela Monastery. This icon which is considered important in the Christian world is today called the icon of "Panagia Soumela" by the Christians. This icon was painted by one the authors of the Bible,namely by Saint Luke. As it is well known, Saint Luke was a great doctor, historian and was famed for being a great iconist in the history of the church with many other icons that he drew apart from the icon of Panagia*

Soumela. According to a common belief and several existing sources, Saint Luke took the icon in Sumela with him wherever he went and this is why Holy Virgin Mary blessed Saint Luke so that may every deed of him be accomplished.

With the execution of Saint Luke in 84 AD on a crucifix set on an olive tree, his loyal disciple Ananias took the icon to Athens. The Icon became very famous all around the Christian world because of the innumerous miracles that it created. A church was built in Thebes near Athens in devotion to it and was placed there.

Then, later in the 4th century while a young priest named Basil was having a service, Virgin Mary appeared to him. Virgin Mary promised him and his nephew Sotirichos that She would stay with them all their lives and told them to do their preparations to become a monk. She told them to go to the monastery of the church where the Icon of Panagia Soumela was placed in Thebes at that time. Thus, they went into the church where the icon was present. As they began praying many angels singing hymns piled in the church and a sweet voice coming from the icon told Basil and Sotirichos said that she would accompany them and guide them through all their lives. Immediately after that, the icon was taken from where it was kept, by the two angels through an open window out of the church as accompanied by hymns.

The icon was taken as such by the angels in a miraculous way to Mount Melaon, the northeast of the Black Sea, situated at an approximate location of 45 km. to the south of Trabzon. The two monks were flabbergasted by what they saw at the church and wondered excitedly where the icon taken out of the window by the angles was gone. After all that Virgin Mary appeared to them again as they prayed in the church and told them to follow the path that She showed them to reach Mount Mela on the northeast of the Black Sea to the south of Trabzon. Virgin Mary appeared to them every night in their dreams and showed them the way to follow.

Then, after that, Basil was given the name "Barnabas" and his nephew Sotirichos was called "Sophronios". According to the legend, these two monks reached Trabzon. When Barnabas and Sophronios reached Trabzon, they began to look for Mount Mela. As they continued to search for the icon of Sumela, they gave a break. A farmer there showed them where Mount Mela was found. The monks began to walk around Mount Mela and legend had it that, the next day they reached the summit of the mountain by following a stream flowing down from mountain and slept at a place close to the peak. When they woke up next morning, they found themselves inside a dry cave close to the peak of that mountain. When they went into it looking for the icon again, as elsewhere, they found the Icon of Panagia Soumela in front of them shining on a flat overhanging spot.

FRESCOS OF SUMELA MONASTERY

The most important section of Sumela is the cave church, also called the main rock church located on one side of the courtyard. This church was constructed by flattening the interior areas of the sacred cave or hollow and closing its outlet with a flat wall.There is a small chapel adjacent to this wall as an overhanging part.

The interior and exterior areas are decorated with fresco paintings in several layers. In some parts, all three layers are clearly visible. The lowest layer is very different and better than the others in terms of its colours and quality. It is seen that the subjects change in each layer, too. The frescos found here have scripts telling that they dated to the years 1710 and 1732. Inside the cave church, on the other hand, there were frescos dating to the period of Alexios III on the wall next to the courtyard. On those frescos, Alexios III was depicted with his two sons Manuel III and Andronikos. None of those portraits reached our time. On the outside a great scene of doom's day carved on the surface of the rock is seen underneath the falling out stucco coating which reached our time only with its surface lines along with other scenes brought to daylight underneath it. Underneath the wall of the small chapel where a dragon and two cavalry Saints (Georgios and Demetrios) were depicted, was two more layers of paintings that were visible. On one part, in the lowest layer were the decorations of a figure in an emperor's suit with a diadem and another figure above it again with a diadem with the scenes of Metamorphosis, that is, the transformation (transfiguration) of Christ on Mount Tabor. It can, then, be said that the old and valuable wall paintings of Sumela Monastery have survived in the lower layers of the walls where the stucco coating did not completely fall away.

Looking at the paints colours in the paintings in both the interior and the exterior sections, it is seen that the colour yellow overrode in most of them with a sharp and defined appearance. The colour that followed yellow was scarlet red and then came a paint which was a mixture of green and pink. The work, the subjects and expressions displayed on the paintings as well as the linking and transmission of the events display the clear signs of a medieval approach of painting.

The most important aspect of the frescos is that they were very finely ornamented on the façades displaying a clear technique of expression.

The fingers of a male's hand in the big painting seen on the ceiling of Main Rock Church are identical with the shape, painting and expression of the fingers of a male hand found in Chora (Kariye) Mosque. The fingers are somewhat deformed and have an unrealistic look in terms of the opening angle and the semi-circular design. And the noses become narrower at the top and wider and longer towards the point with the eyes streching to the sides depicted as if looking at a certain point. The eyebrows are thin with sharp edges and the foreheads are depicted as open and slightly narrow. All of the fingers are long. All of the eyes have been depicted to have the identical look of agony. This technique of painting is also reminiscent of the agonized Jesus and crying Mary of the Medieval Age. The shoulders are depicted as rounded, necks as long, chins sharp and lips thin and puckered.

The paint used in them is the soil paint, the primitive paints used in the production of medieval frescos look like the stone moss paints of the old times. The stucco coatings of the wall are made of a mixture of hay and limestone polished with egg white. Virgin Mary Monastery displays the characteristics of expression, mastery and work that all the other Orthodox temples have. This characteristic of it is based on its trait as being the oldest one on the Black Sea coasts, its unique aspects and its peculiarity of being established on an unknown place in an environment that the nature is adorned in an unprecedented way.

The decoration of frescos in the monasteries and the arrangement of the scenes in a specific order are more difficult here than the other churches having a plan on a certain location. Since the monasteries did not have a certain plan, the frescos might even have to be painted on very challenging rock surfaces and inclined walls. That is why it is difficult to produce a fresco at a monastery wall where the proper story telling in a frame can not be applied very well. The oldest part of Sumela Monastery, the natural cave section, was converted into a church by constructing walls on the north and east. The church was completed with the chapel, added to the eastern wall of the cave church. The ceiling and the interior and the exterior walls of the cave chruch were covered all in frescos. The frescos were painted in different periods, and the three layers of frescos were mostly painted on one another.

After the years that the Sumela Monastery was constructed, it was decorated with frescos as of the

9th century until the second half of the 17th century at different periods of time. The construction date of the frescos that are visible today do not have any harmony in itself and especially there are scenes on the ceiling and interior walls of the cave church dating back to different periods. The stucco coating on which the first layer of frescos was painted, was made of a simple mixture of sand and limestone. On the frescos painted on this coating were the shades of dark green as the dominant colour of the paint.These frescos were thought to have been painted in the 9th century by the famous master Nikoliyos. Hay was used on the second layer in order to make the surface of the fresco stronger. Knurls were opened on the first layer frescos to make the second layer stick on it better. A mixture of burgundy, light brown and pink colours of paint dominated the second layer. These frescos can be seen on the destroyed parts of the third layer on the lower parts of the northern wall of the cave church at the lower parts of the doom's day scene right outside the church. This layer is estimated to have been made in the 14th century.

The third layer of the frescos was produced towards the end of the 17th century. The stucco coating of the third layer frescos is very different from the others. The mixture of this coating looked very much like the Horasan filling, including the pebbles, sand, limestone, hay, egg white and flax and hemp fibers.The colours of this layer displayed a significant development with the use of sharp colours such as burgundy, red, purple, blue, green and golden yellow. When the coating of the third layer was made, symmetrical knurls were opened on the second layer coatings and frescos to make the top layer stick better. Professor of Fine Arts Semavi Eyice says that the frescos were painted in different periods.

As a result of that, the frescos we see in Sumela today are three-layered with different topics made on top of one another, mostly produced in the late 17th century. According to Eyice, the lowest layer is better than the other two in terms of the quality of colours and painting. According to the inscription on the southern door, the third layer frescos were made upon the order of Iqnatius, the Bishop of Chaldia (Gümüşhane) at around 1740.

The frescos of the monastery, especially the depictions of Mary Platytera and Pantakrator Jesus on the ceilings of the church were mostly produced in the Oriental-Eastern style. The flat noses depicted in thick lines and the Mongolian type of eye brows resemble the Oriental-Eastern style. Although the frescos are not too old, their painting style displays the impact of Cappadocia. The third layer of frescos mostly gives the impression that they were painted on the second coating of frescos with a meticulous work by means of copying.

The frescos found in the inner eastern wall of the Cave Church are older than the ones in the front façade. Windows were opened on the eastern wall and as a result of it, the frescos of the interior area were significantly deteriorated and major pieces of some frescos were even lost since they were left inside the window pane that was opened later. No such damage was observed in the front part of the same wall since they were painted after the windows were opened.

When considered a whole, the frescos display significant similarities with the pre-Mongolian period of Russia which is a clear combination of the Byzantine and Slavic arts. The artists painted the exterior of the noses, around and below the eyes of the frescos into reddish brown or dark brown probably for the purpose of making them last longer in a solid shape. The liveliness of the colours of the frescos displayed a continuous development with the colours used in every layer, each of which was richer, sharper and shinier than the other. The liveliness and harmony of the colours in the last layer is perfect. Rice states that the frescos of Sumela had similarites with the Russian art rather than Cappadocia in terms of the colours and the techniques of ornamentation.

The frescos of the Cave Church were painted on the exterior façade, interior walls and chapels and in small chapels in the upper sections of the monks' rooms in a few scenes as well. Two of the frescos in the small chapels, i.e. the killing of the monster by the Saints and the depiction of a deer as a symbol of immortality, survived our time. The first destruction seen on the frescos dated to the 18th century when the number of the visitors of the monastery significantly increased. Those visiting it carved their names and dates of visit on the frescos as a memory and even pulled out and took away some parts of certain depictions since they believed in their sacredness and healing power. On the frescos are the writings and dates from those periods in Russian, Armenian, English, Greek, written in different languages and alphabets.

The passages of the scenes in the front line are embellished with decorations and motifs. While the frescos narrated more than one topic, even the story of a life was fitted into the same scene (as in the life of Prophet Elijah) just like the progressive scenes of the story line of a movie.

Semavi Eyice refers to the research that he conducted in 1962 and his observations of the major destruction of the frescos and the theft of many big pieces as follows: "*... what drew the attention at first sight was the look of a site all over the place as a ruin and that the frescos on the walls were skillfully cut out of their places in orderly square forms and taken away. The achievement of such a difficult thing with a great skill shows that it was not committed by the local people but by the "intellectual" foreign visitors who were keen on such memories and had the back ground on them*"[12]. There were names and dates carved on the frescos scripted with sharp edged materials by visitors both in recent dates and also in the past by the Christian visitors (In 1880, as Tozer also noted, the names and memories carved on the frescos by the visitors with the use of sharp materials were actually not made by Turks but by Greeks (cf. Tozer, ibid.p.441). The main reason for the destruction in recent years was the treasure hunting.

Among those writings that destroyed the frescos are many writings and dates in Greek, Armenian and Russian alphabets Furthermore, some of these date back to the 18th century.

Conclusion

In a research carried out regarding the preference of holiday venues in our country, those preferring Trabzon were asked about the reason for such choice of theirs, and out of the answers given, those who referred to "Sumela Monastery" corresponded to % 47,6. Out of the answers given to another question on the touristic peculiarities of Trabzon, 32% of the respondents mentioned the name of Sumela Monastery making it the most preferred visiting location.[13] This observation was also confirmed by the number of visitors. In 1973, the Sumela monastery was opened for touristic visits.

That time, totally 14000 people visited the monastery i.e. 8000 foreign and 6000 domestic tourists. In 2004, this figure reached 138360 with 22279 (16.1%) foreign and 116081 (83.9%) domestic visitors. In other words, the number of foreign tourists visiting the Monastery between 1973 and 2004 increased by 178.5% while the number of the domestic visitors increased by 1834.7%[14].

Sumela Monastery is a touristic center with an amazing structure diplaying the will of the mankind and natural beauty and the number of its visitors becomes higher and higher as it is better known. Altındere Valley does not allow for the construction of facilities of accomodation in the area with its narrow and steep cliffs and forest land. This is the reason why the construction of roads to enable an access to the site, is impossible. The number of visits increases year by year, as we said above, owing to the number of people who are curious to go there to see the monastery as a miraculous display of the will of mankind again. It may not be an endeavour equaling the will displayed by those who constructed it.

Sumela Monastery is located inside a splendid natural setting at a height of 300 m. from the valley on the ground. We tried to narrate Sumela Monastery here as a small wonderous miracle placed almost inside a hollow on a steep cliff with its importance in terms of history, religion and the people of the region.

When chosing the pictures of specific frescos among all, the criteria behind this choice was preferring those with a total visual integrity and the least damage in terms of reflecting the account in history, instead of using them all. It was very difficult to even read the story told in those frescos that went through serious damage.

Northern Wall of the Cave Church

Apostle Jonah

It is the fresco on the upper left of northern wall showing Him as half-swallowed by a fish. On the horizontally long fresco designed in keeping with the connection of the wall of the cave and the ceiling is a paper in Apostle Jonah's and a halo on His head (fig.35).

Figure 35- Prophet Jonas

Mary Nikopia and Jesus in Bishop's Costumes

These are the second and third frescos of the wall from the left. Mary Nikopia (Holy Bringer of Victory) is shown as holding Her baby son Jesus at the level of Her belly in the scene of Mary Nikopia. In this scene Mary is depicted as the space that does not fit anywhere because of the child Jesus. The third fresco shows Jesus in bishop's cloths as surrounded by clouds. There is a halo on Jesus' head and a cross embroidered on each of His shoulders. The ones in the church are shown as praying (fig.36).

Figure 36- Mary Nikopia and Jesus in Bishop's Gown

Mary on the Throne, Jesus, Holy Trinity (Thetokos Enthronos)

(1a,1b,1c)

The frescos on the east of the northern wall of the Cave church show the splendid depictions of many scenes intermingled with one another. On the right hand side of the scene from the perspective of the onlookers are the figures representing the martyrs or the ones having reached the status of Sainthood, and the bishops in the history of Christianity are shown in two lines with halos. The scene was depicted with great care given to the garments of the Saints and martyrs keeping with the period and geography that they belong to as well as the depiction of the scene as a crowd of figures. On the right side, the kings present the manuscripts in their hands to Mary and Jesus on the throne depicted in their glorious costumes (fig.37-39).

Figure 37- 1a

Figure 38- 1b

Figure 39- 1c

In the most glorious part of the scene is the depiction of Mary who sits on the gilded throne among the clouds with Her child Jesus in Her hands. Child Jesus is barefooted in the scene resembling the icons that represent it. The throne that Mary sits in was depicted in details resembling the Baroque style. Above the scene, right on the top of the head of Mary depicted among a patch of clouds is the Pigeon "Holy Spirit" and right above it on the ceiling is "God" looking like an old man. His two hands are in the position of consecration. There are the depictions of cherubim and high rank angels on both sides of the depiction of God.

The beautifully depicted angels are seen on both sides of Mary sitting on the throne with Jesus. The throne on the clouds is carried by the angels depicted below and on both sides of it. The angels right next to the throne on the left and right hold globes with elliptical shapes in their hands, the angel on the right also wears a cloak in very sharp colours.

Child Jesus sitting on His mother's lap on the throne wears a burgundy cloak over a light green gown with His two hands in the position of consecration. The gilded throne looks shinier as the scene shows that sun lights fall on it from the window up on the eastern wall of the church. There are beautifully-clothed angels on both sides of the throne.

Selection and Appointment of the Apostles by Jesus

In the middle of the fresco is Jesus with His dark burgundy gilded gown and a purple cloak over it. He is holding a paper open in V shape and pinpoints the apostles on the right and left of the frame to appoint them for their posts (fig.40).

Figure 40- Jesus Choosing His Apostles

Bishop and Kings Praying in front of the Icon of Mary and Jesus

On the fresco in the painting on the left is Mary Hodegitria: the icon of Mary the Guide, the Leader with child Jesus in Her arms. On the left of this icon is the icon of Jesus consecrating with His hands. This is the section of the church called Ikonastasis, situated between the section of apsis and naos which cannot be entered by anyone other than the clergymen. In front of the icons are about ten bishops with the symbols of cross on their garments.

On the fresco right above the section that is ascended by four steps is the icon of Jesus on the belly of Mary. Mary who fits the God who cannot be fitted anywhere is called as Mary (Hora tu Ahurito or Kariye Mary). In front of the icon are a king, a bishop and the king's men (fig.41).

Figure 41- Bishops and Kings Worshipping

Cave Church Eastern Wall

On the very top are Jesus, Mary, Saint Joanna and other Saints depicted with wine leaves among the clusters of grapes. Hands of Jesus are depicted in the position of consecration.

Prophet Abraham's Sacrifice of His Son

The fresco appears to have been significantly damaged by the fire of the monastery. It does not look like the other frescos in this section whose conditions are not satisfactory because of the reverse angle of light that they receive.

On the fresco in the second row on the left, Prophet Abraham sacrifices His son (Isaac in Christian faith or Esmail in Muslim faith). They both give an ear to the sound coming from heaven. On the left of the scene are Abraham and His son Isaac walking towards the mountain as they are instructed to do so (fig.42).

Figure 42- Jesus Choosing His Apostles

Jesus' Descencion to the Land of the Dead (Anastasis)

This fresco is different from the classical depictions of Anastasis. From the perspective, Adam and Eve are perceived as standing side by side. Behind Adam and Eve, there are myriads of figures on whose identity we have no idea. Figures on the left must be David, His son Solomon and John, the Baptist. Jesus is in a white mandorla and holds the hands of Adam and Eve. Eve is red from top to toe (fig.43).

Figure 43- Jesus going down to the Land of Dead

Descent of Jesus from the Cross

In this rather vague depiction between two windows there are Nikodim, Joanna and Joseph of Armatia taking Jesus down from the cross. Below are several women depicted as crying (fig.44).

Figure 44- Jesus' being taken down from the Cross

Crucifixion

The fresco was destroyed in fire and also the opening window had a negative impact on it. Upper part of Jesus' body is not seen. There are two angels on both sides of Jesus on the cross. The dominating colour is red. This fresco is more crowded than the other crucifixion scenes and on its left are emirofori, all crying. There are two soldiers in front of Mary. The soldier called Lonikinos is piercing a spear into Jesus' chest. On the right, in front of the crowd are Apostle Joanna and the Captain who had faith in Jesus when He was dying. The figure on the left of the cross serving sour wine with the sponge that he has stuck on a branch of zufa must be Aisopos.

Bread and Wine Communion

It is situated on the right of the window in the second row. On the left He gives bread to the apostles while on the right, He consecrates the apostles who are given wine (fig.45).

Figure 45- Bread and Wine Communion

Washing of the Feet

It is placed to the far right of the second row. Jesus washes and dries the feet of the apostles sitting on the left of the scene. The apostle pointing over his head by his right hand is Petrus (fig.46).

Figure 46- Feet Washing

Abraham and Melchizedek

Figure 47- Abraham and Melchizedek

Prophet King Melchizedek depicted in the standing position offers bread and wine to Prophet Abraham who is kneeling and consecrating him. King Melchizedek has a crown and a halo on his head. His clothes are more ornate in appearance than those of Prophet Abraham. The buidings with the conic domes on the back-ground represent the city of Sodome (fig.47).

Jewish Candelabrum on the Altar

The candelabrum with seven arms is placed on the altar. On both sides of it, are two people with halos on their heads. The other details of the portrait are not clear (fig.48).

Figure 48- Altar, Jewish Candelabrum

Ceiling

Pantakrator Jesus and His Apostles

At the highest point on the ceiling is the depiction of Pantakrator Jesus. Frescos of Pantakrator symbolize the heavenly power of Jesus. There were two cherubim (angels) on both sides of Jesus but the one on the left was destroyed. The depiction is framed by inscriptions. The halo on his head is different from the usual ones. Jesus holding the Bible in his left hand, points at the holy trinity by his right hand. The apostles around the tape of inscriptions are depicted in winged heads (fig.49).

Figure 49- Jesus and the Apostles

Mary Platytera

Figure 50- Jesus and the genealogical tree

This fresco of Mary is located on the ceiling in a gigantic size with her two arms open to the sides and with Jesus on her lap depicted as a child. The depictions of Mary with Jesus on her lap as Theotokos (Mother of God) are called Mary Platytera (fig.50).

Cave Church Southern Wall

Saint Ignatius

It is situated on the southern wall to the right of the depictions of Saint Onouphrios and Saint Iertos. He looks quite solemn although he is being eaten by two lions; one eating his shoulder, the other his foot. He has a cross on each of his shoulders which are the symbols of the rank of a bishop; and he has a halo on his head. The use of colours and the details of the depiction are very clear (fig.51).

Figure 51- Saint Ignatius

Three Frescos

The frescos in this section are in a destroyed condition, the bottom parts of some frescos fell away and colours of some of them were deteriorated. As much as it can be seen though, there are depictions on it showing Mary and Gabriel and Mary between the two angels (fig.52).

Figure 52- Mary between two Angels and visit of Elizabeth

Mary's Visit to Elizabeth

In this depiction, Elizabeth, the aunt of Mary, who is pregnant for John the Baptist and Mary who is pregnant to the fatherless Jesus embrace each other. On the background is the city of the Judas tribe. After that is the fresco next to it (fig.53):

Figure 53- Mary, Elizabeth and Joseph

Mary's Meeting with Joseph

Mary meets her fiancée Joseph. Upon hearing the pregnancy of his fiancée, Joseph gets suspicious. In the painting he is depicted as holding a stick on his left hand and questioning Mary. Mary defends herself saying she is innocent by holding her two hands up in the air. An angel appears to Joseph in his dream and tells him that Mary will give birth to a fatherless child by God and that he should not touch Mary, but not give up marrying her either.

Birth of Jesus and Worshipping of the Shepherds

Jesus lies in the middle in the manger. There is the head of an ox and a horse behind. Mary and Joseph are on the left and right of baby Jesus. On the right are the shepherds who come to worship the baby. Below the manger is a shepherd playing the pipe while his sheep and lamb scatter around (fig.54).

Figure 54- Birth of Jesus and worshipping of shepherds

Angel Leading the Three Prophets and the Worshipping of the Prophets

Three Prophets on the left, Kaspar, Baltazar and Meltior are lined up on their horses in the order of age. They are following the angel who shows them the way. On the right, the prophet's eyes are on the baby. Fresco was seriously damaged because of humidity (fig.55).

Figure 55- Mary guiding the three Prophets

Return of the Three Prophets (left)

Three prophet Kings or soothsayers in gallant clothes wait for their maids to prepare their horses for the return trip (fig.56).

Figure 56- Return of three prophets, escape to Egypt

Escape to Egypt (right)

This Fresco narrates the escape of Joseph to Egypt by taking Jesus and Mary with him after dreaming that he goes after the return of the prophet Kings. Jesus is depicted on the left over the shoulders of Joseph and Mary on a donkey dragged by a servant.

Presentation of Jesus to the Temple and Saint Simon (Hipopant)

On the left side of the depiction is Joseph and Mary with the Prophet Anna. She also has a halo over her head. On the right, Saint Simon gives Jesus back to His mother after the consecration (fig.57).

Figure 57- Jesus being presented to the temple

Cave Church Exterior Façade

Creation of the World (1,2,3,4 from the right)

On the first and second depictions, the earth is empty. There are mountains, valleys and seas. On the third description, God Jesus is depicted as bare-footed, with a beard and a celestial halo inside a golden yellow mandor. He stands in the middle of the earth. From our perspective, on the right is the peacock: the symbol of immortality in shining beams. The heavenly halo on the head of the peacock is something that is never seen apart from Jesus. The celestial halo represented by the letters of alfa and omega is only used for Jesus. On the fourth depiction to the far left is the son on the top with the moon and the stars on the left. The son is depicted as smiling. The son with the smiling human face lights and warms several animals on earth (fig.58-61).

Figure 58- Creation of World

Figure 59- Creation of World

Figure 60- Creation of World; Christ and symbol of immortality Peacock in shinning Mandorla

Figure 61- Creation; animals on earth under the sun, moon and star

Creation of Adam and Eve (5,6)

Jesus is depicted as clad in the 3rd fresco, i.e. the creation of the world. He is shown as leaning on Adam with a celestial halo on his head. He is witnessing the creation of Adam or he is creating Him. The naked Adam is smiling. There are two storeys on the fresco on the right; while on the left side, Adam is depicted as sitting and counting the names of the animals in front of Him. To the right of the depiction is Jesus creating Eve out of the rib of sleeping Adam (fig.62-63).

Figure 62- Creation of Adam

Figure 63- Adam is sitting left, specifying animals, Christ and creation of Eve. Wall is border of Heaven

Eating of the Forbidden Fruit (7,8)

This is a depiction with two narratives, too. On the left are Adam and Eve standing in front of Jesus as naked. On the right Eve is eating from the forbidden fruit and is thus deceived by the serpent. The serpent is depicted in green color and wrapped around the tree. On the next depiction to the right of the window, tempted by Eve, Adam is eating from the forbidden fruit (fig.64-65).

Figure 64- Adam and Eve in the presence of Christ after eating forbidden fruit

Figure 65- Adam is alone eating fruit

Inquiry and Dismissal from Heaven (9)

On the left, Jesus is interrogating Adam and Eve for having eaten the forbidden fruit. Eating of the forbidden fruit as a sin leads to the feeling of shame and they cover themselves with fig leaves. On the right is a very successful depiction of Jesus, an angel with a weapon and the expression of an astonishment on the faces of Adam and Eve as they are dismissed from heaven (fig.66).

Figure 66- (at the left side); Adam and Eve chastised by Christ, (right side); Christ and a cherub expel Adam and Eve from Heaven

Adam and Eve on Earth (10)

A fresco with three storeys: On the far left, at the gate of Heaven are two Cherubim (angels) with weapons in both hands preventing humanbeings from coming back. In the middle is Eve weaving wool and on the right is Adam ploughing a plow with double oxen (fig.67).

Figure 67- On the earth; (left side), Adam and Eve wearing skin garment. (Right side); Adam ploughs with two bulls, Eve spinning wool

Resurrection of Jesus and the Sleeping Soldiers (11)

Figure 68- The Resurrection and sleeping soldiers

Jesus is ascending to heaven by scattering lights among triangular clouds and his right hand is doing the consecration while holding on his left hand a spear ornamented in crosses which symbolize victory in the Byzantine art. On his feet are the stigmata.

Jehovah is the captain running away with the fear of Jesus resurrecting while the other soldiers are sleeping. Below the figure of Jesus is the cover of the dark green sarcophagus depicted as falling back downwards. The buildings on the right of Jesus symbolize the city while the women symbolize the public (fig.68).

Incredulous Thomas (12)

Jesus is larger than His apostles. He has marks of wounds on his hands, feet and chest. Thomas suspecting that he has Jesus in front of him, is touching the wounds on His chest. Thomas and the five apostles are depicted on the right of Jesus, while the rest of the apostles are seen on the left. No one was chosen to replace the traitor Jehovah yet (fig.69).

Figure 69- The doubting Thomas

Empty Grave and the Women (13)

The figure on the left whose head is destroyed, is Gabriel. He is pointing at the empty grave and telling the women that He is resurrected as he has left the sarcophagus. Mary Magdalene, Jacob's mother, Mary and Salome are watching in amazement the shroud and the clothes inside the empty sargophagus, out of which Jesus resurrects.

On the right is Mary Magdalene telling what is happening to Saint Petrus(fig.70).

Figure 70- Women in the empty Tombs

Council of Nicaea (14)

Figure 71- İznik (Nicaea) Council

The portrait tells about the 7th Council held in Nicaea (İznik). This is the biggest fresco seen on this wall. The portrait depicting the council with Patriarche Tarasios, the head of the 7th Ecumenical Council, the bishops and the monks is quite successful. It seems as if the arguments of that time are still valid today (fig.71).

Jesus and the Woman of Samaria (15)

Jesus is sitting on the left by the well. He is speaking with the Samaritan woman who is there to fill water from the well. The apostles coming back from the city with food are listening to them. The settlement on the right inside the city walls must be Samirne (fig.72).

Figure 72- Christ and the Samaritan women

Opening of the Eyes of the Blind Man (16)

Jesus is depicted as leaning on a man who was born blind and touching his eyes with the apostles on the back-ground. He may be putting mud on the eyes of the man. The blind man is going to the pool of Shiloam to wash his face upon the instruction of Jesus (fig.73).

Figure 73- Opening of blind's eyes

Cain Killing His Brother Abel and Getting Rid of the Demon (18)

First murder: On the top, Cain's murdering his brother Abel is depicted. Cain is stepping on his brother's belly with one foot and hitting him with the stick in his right hand. Out of the offerings of the two brothers in a chest, the fire burns Abel's offering but does not accept that of Cain. The flocks of the two brothers are depicted at the back and on the sides.

On the left bottom part are Jesus and his eight apostles. Black ginnies come out of the mouths of naked men with ginnies. The ginnies mixed with the pigs in the flock jump along with the pigs into the lake that is drawn in black colour. On top are two well-dressed shepherds watching what is going on (fig.74).

Figure 74- (Top) Cain is killing Abel, (Below) Driving out the demons

Fiftieth Day(Pentikosti)

Pentikosti is one of the last depictions in which Mary is seen. It is not mentioned in the Bible. Pentikosti means the fiftieth in Greek. It is the feast held fifty days after the Easter when Mary and the apostles remind the believers of the descent of the Holy Spirit (fig.75).

Figure 75- 50th Day

Metamorphosis

Jesus is in white clothes on Mount Tabor. He is ascending to the heaven inside a mandorla surrounding an octagonal stellar form by scattering lights all around, and thus transforms from the human nature into a celestial nature. The transforming Jesus is consecrating with His right hand and is holding a pile of papers in the other. On both sides of Jesus are depictions of the Apostles Moses and Elijah. Apostles Jacob and Joanna are grovelled down in fear while Petrus stands up and talks with Jesus (fig.76).

Figure 76- Metamorphosis

Prophet Elijah

Elijah is in the city of Tishbe in Gilead. He was appointed by God as a messenger to go and tell the Pagan King Ahab of Samaria that there would be no rain in the upcoming years until He orders so. There was no rain there anymore. On the far left of the depiction are the public begging the King and the Queen Isabel for rain. On the right next to it is the Prophet Elijah on Mount

Carmel, Ahab and 450 prophets offering victims to the Gods in front of the public. According to the deal, the first offerings would be given by the Pagan prophets to their own Gods and then by Prophet Elijah to His God. The offerings of Pagan prophets are not burnt by their Gods. The bull which is the offering of Elijah is burnt by God on an altar made of twelve stones. So, Elijah urges the public to kill the Pagan prophets.

The figure on the right is Elijah who is afraid of Ahab's wife hiding behind a desert shrub and falling asleep. An angel brings a jug of water and food to the sleeping Elijah. Elijah leaves Gilead with Elisha and they set out for the road. Upon reaching the River Jordan, Elijah takes off His cloak and hits it on the water and the waters are divided into two. They walk across the river as such. As they walk, a chariot of fire comes from heaven and separates them by taking Elijah away with a storm. Elijah's cloaks drop as he flies to heaven. Elisha takes the cloak and never sees Elijah again. Elijah is in a chariot driven by a pair of winged horses (fig.77-78).

Figure 77- Prophet Elijah

Figure 78- Prophet Elijah

Exorcism

The old man is in his bed. As the little devil drawn in dark colours runs away down the frame, the bigger devil depicted in gray colour is trying to stab the man with the spear in His hand. On the right hand side are four women. One of them is chasing the devil away, while the others are standing and watching what is going on (fig.79).

Figure 79- Exorcism

Ascension of Jesus

Jesus is sitting inside his elliptical mandorla carried by the angels. At the bottom are the eleven apostles and Mary. No one was chosen to replace the traitor Jehovah (fig.80).

Figure 80- Ascension of Jesus

Chapel Exterior

Mary's Evangelismos

Figure 81- Mary learning the good news

In the depiction are Gabriel and Mary. The gospel tells about Virgin Mary's becoming pregnant by the power of God. Gabriel tells Mary that she is chosen by God and will give birth to Jesus (fig.81).

Resurrecting of Lazarus (The Egersis Lazarus)

Jesus with the celestial halo on His head is resurrecting Lazarus who died four days ago, by consecrating him with His right hand. Seven of his apostles are following Him. On the right is Lazarus getting out of the sarcophagus that he is buried in as his sisters Martha and Mary are opening the lid of the sarcophagus. Neighbours of Martha and Mary are watching the scene on the back ground (fig.82).

Figure 82- Lazarus' Resurrection

Jesus Enters Jerusalem

In the portrait, the halos on the heads of the apostles are depicted in different colours.It is not known whether the use of different colours has a special meaning.

Jewish tax-gatherer Zacchaeus wishes to see Jesus but fails because he is short and therefore climbs the tree. Walking under that tree Jesus tells Zacchaeus to come down from the tree and that he will stay at his house that night. In Zacchaeus' house, Jesus asks His apostles to find him a black foal. And He enters Jerusalem riding on that foal. Jesus is depicted as consecrating with his right hand on the foal and the joyful crowd welcoming him is depicted as spreading their clothes on the rope that the foal passes (fig.83).

Figure 83- Jesus enters Jerusalem

David and His Son Solomon

In the middle of the pediment is the Prophet King David, with the royal crown and a halo on his head, gathering the people of Israel who were scattered all around (only their heads are seen in the picture). On his right is the son of Prophet David, Solomon again with a crown and a halo on his head, who was enthroned after his father (fig.84).

Figure 84- David and his son Solomon

Washing of Feet

Jesus is depicted in the middle on his knees as washing the feet of the Apostle Petrus. Petrus is pointing at his head asking Jesus to wash and consecrate his head as well. On the right are the apostles depicted as renouncing Jesus's washing of the feet of Petrus (fig.85).

Figure 85- Feet Washing

Jesus in front of Governor Pilatus

Jesus is in the middle of the depiction with a halo on His head between the two soldiers who are holding Him. Pilate is sitting on his throne. The figures behind Jesus must be the member of the high consul who blames Jesus, seen only in the parts of their feet due to the damage.

Governor Pilate asks Jesus "Are you the king of the Jews?" He answers "Yes" and does not answer any other question. In every Passover, a convict chosen by the public is forgiven. People are asked if they choose Jesus or convict Barabas. Due to the provocations by the prophets and the old men, Barabas is chosen. They ask Jesus to be crucified. Pilate gives Jesus to the soldiers to be crucified (fig.86).

Figure 86- Jesus and Governor Pilatus

Jesus Wearing the Crown of Thorns

Jesus is depicted as larger in size than the figures around Him. He is in a red gown that the soldiers made Him wear. In His right hand is a reed given by the soldiers. The soldiers carry on the torture by putting a crown of thorns on Jesus' head. The crown of thorns is seen underneath the halo.

Here, normally, there have to be the depictions of Jesus being crucified and taken down from the cross. But those depictions could not be used due to the heavy damage they underwent (fig.87).

Figure 87- Jesus' crown of thorns

Interment of Jesus

In the middle of the depiction is the cross leaning on the stairs. Jesus is placed in the sarcophagus on a linen cloth. Dark green sarcophagus is ornamented and He will be resurrecting inside the same sarcophagus. Jesus' mother is holding His head on Her lap and she is crying as Her own head leant onto His. The other two figures of Mary are lamenting behind Jesus. Apostle Joanna is kissing Jesus' hand. Nikodimos and Joseph are sad as they are placing Jesus inside the sarcophagus. There are two angles on the left and the right (fig.88).

Figure 88- Burial of Jesus

Northern Rock

Doom's Day

It is believed that Jesus will definitely come back to earth one day to judge all dead or alive. In the depictions of the Doom's day, Jesus is seen in the middle on his throne (hetimasia). Thc doom's day depiction here is in three strips painted on top of one another just like the classical doom's day depictions. The strip at the top shows Jesus in the middle on His throne in a mandorla. His mother, John the Baptist, the Apostles, the Saints and angels are seen on the left and right of Jesus. On the depiction of the last trial, those who were good in their lives would go to heaven and those who were bad would go to hell.

At the bottom are the apostles sitting on their thrones. On the left of hetimasia are John the Baptist and Mother Mary asking for the intercession of Jesus for His forgiveness for humanity on the Doom's day.

Left hand side of the third line is the depiction of heaven and the right hand side is hell. Very little of the right part is clear due to heavy damage (fig.89).

Figure 89- Doom's Day

Holy Cross Chapel

The frescos in this section were vulnerable to less damage by human hands in comparison to the sections that are open for visit.

Mary Platytera and the Fathers of the Church

When Jesus is depicted as sitting on His mother's lap on the throne, these depictions are called "Mary Platytera" which means Theotokos(mother of God).

Four fathers of the church are depicted on the vault of the cradle at the bottom of the fresco (fig.90).

Figure 90- Church fathers and saints

Mary Hora Tu Ahurito

The frescos where baby Jesus is depicted on Mary's lap at the level of her belly are called the icons of "Hora Tu Ahurito".

Figure 91- Mary Hora Tu Ahurito

Additionally, if the child Jesus is depicted at the level of His mother's shoulder, as leaning on Her shoulder, these icons are called "Hodigitria Mary" (guide of the church) (fig.91).

Ascension of Jesus

Jesus is sitting inside his elliptical mandorla carried by the angels. The eleven apostles and Mary are seen at the bottom (fig.92).

Figure 92- Ascension of Jesus

Cricifixion of Jesus (Stavrosis)

Jesus' head is on the crucifix with His head slightly bent towards left. He is depicted with the tag of "King of the Jews" that Pilate puts on His head, His mother and Joanna. Especially the astonishment on Mary and Joanna's faces and the crying expression of Joanna were very well depicted (fig.93).

Figure 93- Cricifixion of Jesus (Stavrosis)

Resurrection of Jesus and the Sleeping Soldiers

Jesus holding the cross that symbolizes victory in His hand resurrects in His grave and sits up. He is inside an orange mandorla. The soldiers are sleeping while the sergeant, who is scared, is running away (fig.94).

Figure 94- Resurrection of Jesus and the sleeping soldiers

Baptising of Jesus (Genesis)

He is baptised by his cousin John in the River Sherin. After baptising, Jesus flies to heaven and the soul of God comes and sets on His shoulder in the form of a pigeon. The voice from heaven says, "This is my son, and I am well pleased with him" (fig.95).

Figure 95- Baptising of Jesus Christ

Cherubim (Angels)

On the left side depicted inside a niche in a simple form and in one single colour is the depiction of the cherubim (angels) (fig.96).

Figure 96- Interment of Jesus

REFERENCES

Fallmerayer, Jakob Philp, *Doğu'dan Fragmanlar (Fragments from the East)*, Tr.Salihoğlu, Hüseyin, İmge Pub. 2002.

Fallmerayer, Jakob Philip, *Trabzon İmparatorluğunun Tarihi (History of Trabzon Empire)*, TTK, 2011.

Eyice, Semavi, *TTK Belleten*, Vol. 30 no: 118, 1966.

Eyüpoğlu, İsmet Zeki, *Maçka*, Pencere Publication, 2004.

Köse, İsmail, *4000 Yıllık Mirasın Kutsal İzleri Trabzon*, Akademi Kitapevi, Trabzon 2009.

Mollamehmetoğlu. A.Ş. *Cumhuriyet Newspaper*, July 26, 2003.

Özen Hamiyet, Sürül Ayça, *Sumela Manastırının Değişen Yüzü (The Changing Face of Sumela Monastery)*, Arredamento Architecture, Vol. 01, 2005.

panagiasumela.org

Şen, Ömer, *Trabzon Tarihi*, Derya Kitapevi. Trabzon, 1998.

Urgan, Mina, *Bir Dinazorun Gezileri*, YKY Publications, 1999.

Yaraslı, Göker Yarkın, *Destinasyon İmajı ve Trabzon Yöresine Dönük Bir Çalışma*, Graduate Thesis, Baskent University Institute of Social Sciences.

Zehiroğlu, A. Mican, *Prokopius'un Trabzon Seyahati*, Tarih ve Toplum Dergisi, vol.200, August 2000.

Zaman, Mehmet.http://e-dergi.atauni.edu.tr/ataunisosbil/article/view/1020000213.

NOTES

1 Alicin Monastery of Kızılcahamam/Ankara, was constructed on the slope of a steep cliff like Sumela.

2 Zehiroğlu, A. Mican, Prokopius'un Trabzon Seyahati (Prokopius' Trabzon Travel, *Tarih ve Toplum*, August 2000,vol.200.

3 Fotiadis, Konstantinos, *Die İslamiesirung Kleinasiens und Die Kryptochristen Des Pontos*, Tubingen 1985'ten aktaran Şen, Ömer, *Trabzon Tarihi*, Trabzon 1998.

4 Şen, Ömer.*Trabzon Tarihi (The History of Trabzon)*.Derya Kitapevi. Trabzon 1998.

5 Eyüpoğlu İ.Z. *Maçka*, Pencere Pub.2004, p.70.

6 Cited from Sebahattin Eyüpoğlu: Mollamehmetoğlu. A.Ş. *Cumhuriyet*, July 26, 2003.

7 Fallenmayer, J. *Doğu'dan Fragmanlar (Fragments from the East)*, Tr. Salihoğlu.H. İmge Pub. 2002.

8 Eyice, S. *Trabzon Yakınlarında Kutsal Bakire (Sümela) Manastırı, (Virgin Mary (Sumela) Monastery Near Trabzon)* TTK Belleten, Vol.30,p.243.

9 Fotiadis, K. *Die İslamiesirung Kleinasiens und Die Kriptochristen des Pontos*.Türbingen 1985'ten aktaran Şen, Ömer.*Trabzon Tarihi (History of Trabzon*). Derya Bookstore. Trabzon. 1998 ss:277

10 Zehiroğlu, A. "Mican, Prokopius' Travel to Trabzon", *Tarih ve Toplum*, August 2000,volume:200

11 Eyüpoğlu, *ibid.*

12 Eyice. *ibid* p. 256

13 Yaraslı Göker Yarkın, *Destinasyon İmajı ve Trabzon Yöresine Dönük Bir Çalışma (A Study on Destination Image and Trabzon Region)*, Graduate Thesis,BaşkentUniversity, Social Sciences Institute.

14 Zaman, Mehmet.http://e-dergi.atauni.edu.tr/

FIGURES